D1080460

The Handbook of Running

The Handbook of
Running

Nick Troop and Steven Seaton

PELHAM BOOKS

LONDON

PELHAM BOOKS

Published by the Penguin Group
27 Wrights Lane, London W8 5TZ
Viking Penguin Inc., 375 Hudson Street, New York,
New York 10014, USA
Penguin Books Australia Ltd, Ringwood, Victoria, Australia
Penguin Books Canada Ltd, 10 Alcorn Avenue, Toronto,
Ontario, Canada M4V 3B2
Penguin Books (NZ) Ltd, 182–190 Wairau Road,
Auckland 10, New Zealand

Penguin Books Ltd, Registered Offices: Harmondsworth,
Middlesex, England

First published 1997
10 9 8 7 6 5 4 3 2 1

Typeset in Stone serif by Susan Clarke, Reading
Printed and bound by Bookprint, Barcelona, Spain
A CIP catalogue record for this book is available from the
British Library

ISBN 0 7207 2064 8

Contents

Acknowledgements

Contributors

Tim Turner is the Assistant Editor of *Runner's World* magazine.

Harry Wilson coached Steve Ovett to Olympic 800m gold in Moscow and continues to advise a number of international athletes.

Jack Buckner was the 1986 European 5,000m champion and won bronze over the same distance in the 1987 World Championships.

Hugh Jones has won a number of international marathons, including the 1982 London Marathon, and most recently claimed the Veteran title of the 1995 New York City Marathon.

Joe Dunbar is an applied physiologist who has advised Olympic and World Champions in six different sports. He is also a sub four-minute miler and international distance runner.

Dr Patrick Milroy is a medical adviser to the British Athletic Federation and specialises in running injuries. He is also a 2:25 marathon runner.

Peta Bee is a member of the Sports Nutrition Foundation and a former Junior international distance runner.

Steve Smythe is the race editor of *Runner's World* magazine and a veteran of over fifty marathons, with a best of 2:29.

Karin Zeitvogel is an experienced freelance journalist specialising in ultra-distance and multi-sports events.

Illustrations

All the line drawings are by Raymond Turvey. Copyright for the photographs is held by the following:

David Hewitson: p.68

Robert Howard: p.69

Hulton Getty Collection: pp.1, 4

Mike King: pp.20, 30, 54

Rodale Press/Steven Seaton: pp.6, 7, 9, 13, 27, 28, 31, 37, 46, 48, 63, 65, 67, 73, 77, 82, 83, 90, 92, 105, 114, 118, 120, 125, 129, 132, 137, 139

Sporting Pictures: pp.11, 43

Foreword

I am delighted to endorse *The Handbook of Running*, which draws not only on the broad experience of Nick Troop and Steven Seaton, respectively Publisher and Editor of the excellent *Runner's World* magazine, but also on the matchless expertise in their different fields of Joe Dunbar and Hugh Jones; Harry Wilson and Jack Buckner; Dr Patrick Milroy, and many others.

The Handbook of Running is the latest addition to a highly respected series of books that covers sports as diverse as climbing, riding, swimming, golf and tennis. The philosophy behind the series is that if you really want to master a sport it helps to have all the information in one place, and, with sections on stretching and shoes; marathons and cross-country; cross-training and nutrition, to name a few, *The Handbook of Running* aims to provide everything you need.

Whatever people say about the merits of various sports, for me running is the most natural and fundamental of them all: as St Paul once wrote 'forgetting all that lies behind me, and straining forward to what lies in front, I am racing towards the finishing-point.' I have run for well over half my life, and it is now an integral part of my daily routine. It has changed my life and I hope that, with the help and guidance provided in this book, it will do the same for you.

Sebastian Coe OBE, MP
Editorial Adviser, *Runner's World* magazine
March 1997

1 History

At the 16-mile point during one of his first races, with 10 miles to go to the finish, 1972 Olympic Marathon champion Frank Shorter joked: 'Why couldn't Pheidippides have died *here*?' His comment neatly summed up the legend that surrounds the most famous run of all time in 490 BC – the fatal effort of Athenian runner Pheidippides in conveying the good news to Athens that the invading Persians had been defeated on the plain of Marathon.

Actually, the truth may be somewhat different – whatever distance Pheidippides *did* run, it surely was not the now universally accepted 'marathon' of 26 miles 385 yards! Although the legend has it that Pheidippides arrived with just enough breath to utter the words 'Rejoice, we conquer!' before dying, there are no

Pheidippides delivers news of victory and drops dead on the spot.

1

contemporary reports. Herodotus, writing some fifty years after the Battle of Marathon, has Pheidippides, a trained runner or *hemerodromoi*, running from Athens to Sparta to summon help – a distance of approximately 136 miles, reached 'on the very next day'. There is no mention of any return to Athens until the first-century AD writings of Plutarch.

However, the legend was firmly implanted in the mind of every Greek, and, more importantly, in the minds of the men planning to re-create the Olympic Games of Ancient Greece, Baron Pierre de Coubertin, and his right-hand man, Sorbonne professor Michel Breal.

It was Breal who, accompanying de Coubertin on a trip to Greece to meet the local organising committee and to raise funds, decided that there must be an event to capture the public's imagination. Certainly no race of longer than about three miles had ever formed part of the original Olympic programme. Breal decided on a race to 'revive the famous run of the Marathon soldier', the local organising committee agreed, and the rest, as they say, is history.

Except that, of course, a race between sixteen men over a 40-kilometre distance 100 years ago does not entirely explain the popularity of the marathon distance – or, indeed, recreational and fitness running – today. But it is a starting point, a ripple that had the effect of raising the profile of distance running in a way that had never been done before.

The winner of the 1896 Olympic Marathon, the Greek Spiridon Louis, staggered across the line in 2 hours 58 minutes to become a national hero. He never ran another race, but accepted the plaudits – including free shaves for life from a local barber – from a grateful nation. Louis was no beginner, though: it transpired that he ran beside his water cart from his village to Athens every day,

covering about 28 kilometres. He was undoubtedly the best-prepared man in the race.

Just five months later, the New York City Knickerbocker Athletic Club staged a 25-mile race from Stamford, Connecticut to the Columbia Oval in New York. The race was held in muddy conditions and included many hills, which accounted for the winner, John McDermott, finishing in 3 hours 25 minutes, almost half an hour slower than Louis had done in the Olympics. From this first 'marathon' in the western hemisphere came the race which recently celebrated its centenary – the Boston Marathon, run on Patriots Day in April to celebrate the American revolutionary battle of Lexington in 1775. In 1996 40,000 runners from around the globe lined up in the seventeenth-century village of Hopkinton to make their way back to the city centre. In 1897, a mere fifteen starters, including New York winner McDermott ran the 39 kilometres from Ashland to finish in Exeter Street. Despite leg cramps at 20 miles, McDermott won by over seven minutes in 2 hours 55 minutes, to vow at the finish 'Never again'. How many modern marathoners have uttered those same words! (In fact McDermott returned the following year to finish fourth – despite running 13 minutes faster.)

The Olympic Marathon of 1900 in Paris is best forgotten – indeed the champion, Michel Theato, did not officially know he had won for 12 years! – and there were only eight finishers in a race run in astounding heat. Yet the marathon bug had taken hold and over the next few years races were staged in Switzerland, Austria and South Africa. Britain's first marathon was in Coventry over 25 miles on 9 May 1908, the year of the Olympic Marathon in London that will forever be known as Dorando's race. This was also the first time that the now standard distance of 26 miles 385 yards was used, allegedly to ensure that the finish could be directly beneath the royal box at the White City stadium. Italian Dorando Pietri, an experienced runner, went into the lead at the 25-mile point on a warm and humid afternoon, closely followed by a trio of Americans which included eventual winner John Hayes. Entering the stadium on his own, Pietri, overcome with heat and exhaustion, stumbled several times before being helped over the line, and, inevitably, disqualified. Hayes finished 32 seconds behind but became Olympic champion in 2 hours 55 minutes. Hayes and Pietri both turned professional and raced against each other in America, once at Madison Square Garden in New York, running 260 times around a wooden track. Pietri won by 80 yards.

Professional running – and the gambling that accompanied it – became a lucrative business for all concerned. But gambling had actually played its part earlier in establishing running in the UK. Foot racing, or pedestrianism, is mentioned in Samuel Pepys's diary, specifically a match between the Duke of Richmond's footman and a tiler who was a famous runner. Servants running while their masters placed bets was an increasingly common occurrence, and by the 1750s races were taking place in the Artillery Ground in London, and promoters even charged entry fees for spectators.

However, long-distance races were equally lucrative: Foster Powell ran from London to York and back, a total of 402 miles, in 5 days 18 hours in 1773.

Captain Barclay – actually a Scottish landowner called Robert Barclay Allardice – was a formidable pedestrian. In his prime more than ten thousand people went to see him walk 1,000 miles in 1,000 consecutive hours to earn £16,000. He later turned to running, and was unbeaten in a series of races from 440 yards to 2 miles.

During the first half of the nineteenth century the growing industrialisation of England led to the strongholds of pedestrianism shifting from gentlemen's clubs to public houses in the major cities. This professional clique – despite being rife with corruption and cheating – nevertheless was largely responsible for laying the foundations of the modern track meetings. By the 1850s a dozen purpose-built running tracks were in use in major cities – the first, a two-man track round the cricket ground at Lord's, in 1837. Championship cups and belts began to be offered for the most popular distances – 110 yards, 440 yards, 880 yards, 1 mile, 2 miles, 4 miles, 6 miles, 10 miles – and for jumping.

While the sport was being professionalised in this way, the amateur revolution was also underway at certain universities. At Exeter College, Oxford, in 1850 a strange 'foot grind' race – twenty-four runners taking on twenty-four fences over a two-mile course – was staged by those dispirited by their lack of riding skill in the college steeplechase, and other colleges followed suit, as did Cambridge University. In 1861, Jack MacDonald, a Cambridge solicitor and athletics adviser, brought the famous American runner Deerfoot to Cambridge. Deerfoot (a native American called Louis Bennett) won a six-mile race in front of the Prince of Wales.

Athletics was gaining a new respectability, and clubs started springing up – the first in London was the Mincing Lane Athletic Club, founded in 1863, although Liverpool AC had been formed the year before. It was this latter group who on 14 June 1862 organised an 'Olympic Festival', with events ranging from walking and running races to throwing the cricket ball and gymnastics. Further festivals were held in 1864 and

1865, and in 1864 the first athletics Blues match between Oxford and Cambridge took place.

It was the Liverpool committee's decision to form a National Olympian Society that sent shock waves through athletics organisers in London, who promptly formed the Amateur Athletic Club, which held its first 'annual champion games' on the day before the Boat Race in 1866. The programme of events devised by committee member John Graham Chambers has remained basically the same until the present day – of the eleven events in the first championships of 1866, nine are still Olympic events today. But the roots of the modern running boom of the 1970s and 1980s are not totally explained by the activities of a few elite athletes, although American Frank Shorter's victory in the 1972 Olympic Games marathon is regarded by many as a watershed moment.

After humble beginnings, professional running offered championship cups and belts by the mid-nineteenth century. This is Oxford versus Cambridge.

Rather more directly for the average person, the efforts of US coach Bill Bowerman (who also invented the 'waffle' outsole which appeared on many on the early Nike shoes) were hugely significant several years earlier.

Bowerman himself had been influenced by visiting New Zealand in 1962 with the University of Oregon world record four-mile relay team. Out on a run with his New Zealand counterpart, Arthur Lydiard, Bowerman found that his own fitness, aged fifty, in no way measured up to that of his companion. Following this experience, he began to jog regularly, continuing to do so when he returned to the USA. There in 1967 he published his volume *Jogging*, which became an international bestseller. Another American, Dr Ken Cooper, was equally influential in his promotion of basic exercise for health. *Aerobics*, first published in 1968, explained how ordinary people could improve the quality – and length – of their lives by exercising at a relatively modest level for just 20 minutes, three times a week.

When the New York Road Runners Club changed its marathon course in 1976 from five-laps around Central Park where only 275 had finished the year before, to a point-to-point course through the five boroughs to celebrate the USA's bicentennial, 2,000 starters turned up. Other US marathons experienced the same growth, reacting differently: New York accepted all comers; Boston imposed a time restriction to exclude the slower runners.

In 1979, fifty-year-old journalist and 1956 Olympic steeplechase champion, Chris Brasher, ran the New York City Marathon. It inspired him to think that the same kind of event could happen in London – and, through his determination, it did, in 1981, with over 7,000 starters and 6,418 finishers. Now an established event with over 35,000 accepted to run each year, the London Marathon is the sport's showcase event, along with Newcastle's Great North Run, started by Olympic runner Brendan Foster in 1981. And, while the marathon boom may be over, the number of runners training and competing for other distances is huge. *Runner's World* publishes details of over 3,000 races – from mile to marathon – each year. As a way to get and stay in shape, the words of Bill Bowerman from thirty years ago still ring true: 'Just open your door, and you're in business.'

Why run?

Thirty years ago, if you'd looked at runners lining up for the start of a race you'd have seen roughly the same sort of people you see today at the front of the field – natural runners, with slim builds, not much body fat and efficient cardiovascular and muscular systems. But, thirty years ago, there would have been no one lining up behind those natural runners, a far cry from today when people of all shapes and sizes have trained to run virtually every distance you can think of. Even the marathon, once the preserve of the elite, has fallen to the recreational and fitness runner – incredibly, over 250,000 people have competed in the London Marathon since its inception in 1981. The 'jogging boom' of the early 1980s brought thousands of new people into running, all with their own aims and ambitions. Many of them are still running, and they are joined all the time by countless others.

So why run? Well, research shows that exercisers live longer than non-exercisers, and the most recent research concludes that running is one of the best types of exercise. It's cheap, accessible, time-efficient and burns a lot of calories – it's almost impossible to run and *not* get a

Running just 5–10 miles per week reduces your risk of heart disease by 20 per cent.

vigorous workout. And vigorous is what the latest research says exercise should be: according to a recent study published in the *Journal of the American Medical Association*, 'vigorous exercise' alone increases longevity, meaning running at least 15 miles a week at 10-minute/mile pace or faster. But if you're not simply trying to live longer, maybe you just want to lose a few pounds? Well, you're going to live longer anyway! The ongoing Harvard Alumni Health Study in the USA has the answer: the most recent results of this long-term study show that the thinnest alumni lived the longest, with the thinnest one-fifth having a 40 per cent lower mortality risk than the heaviest one-fifth. And how are you going to lose this weight? Run, of course.

By running just 5–10 miles per week, your risk of heart disease, the UK's number one killer, is reduced by 20 per cent. Studies show that those who run 25–30 miles per week live on average two years longer than their sedentary counterparts. Even if you take up running in your sixties or seventies, you can trim your blood-fat levels and reduce the risk of heart disease. But not only are you going to live longer, your quality of life will be significantly enhanced as well. You'll look and feel better – and your mood will improve. Studies have shown that a 15-minute bout of exercise can be better than a tranquilliser for relieving tension, due to the release of endorphins – chemicals in the brain which limit pain and make you feel calmer.

In fact, running can affect almost all of your body's functions, and usually for the better. Here's how:

Ageing: Recent studies have shown that your physical decline is just 2–5 per cent per decade. The fact that it is more pronounced in older people is because of inactivity. If you run regularly between the ages of forty and fifty, you may lose as little as 2 per cent of your capacity, and if you increase your fitness training over that time, you may even get fitter.

Body fat levels: The average man has 22 per cent body fat, the average woman 27 per cent – levels that running can reduce quickly. Running even three times per week for 30 minutes each session can burn over 1,300 calories per week – a possible 17 pounds of body fat lost in a year. And increasing mileage can significantly add to that loss.

Bones: Moderate amounts of running tend to increase bone thickness in the feet and legs, but high-mileage runners (running over 50 miles per week) can have thinner spines, for reasons which aren't yet clear. If you are training at this level make sure you do some weight training exercises which stress the spine, in order to strengthen it.

Running can improve almost all of your body's functions.

Women runners who train heavily are at risk from osteoporosis in later life. Osteoporosis (literally 'porous bones') is the disease which causes the majority of broken bones in elderly people, and women are eight times more likely to suffer from it. Women trainers can find that their periods stop during times of heavy training (called amenorrhoea), and they are particularly at risk, since amenorrhoea reduces bone density. The answer is to maintain a sufficient calcium intake, and to get regular medical check-ups if you go more than a few months without having a period.

Brain: Besides the release of endorphins – responsible for the so-called 'runner's high', a sense of calm and wellbeing – studies have shown that running can enhance mental functioning: maths and reasoning test scores are higher if done after training sessions.

Circulation: During exercise most of your body's organs and tissues, except those directly used, are drained of blood. However, during recovery, it's the opposite story: arteries and veins expand to cope with the higher volume of blood, and direct this blood to any organ which needs it.

Electrolyte balance: Running can improve blood flow to the kidneys, which allows them to keep better tabs on blood electrolyte levels and decrease the risk of deficiencies.

Regular running, especially in heat, also leads to a reduction in the quantity of electrolytes dissolved in sweat, which lowers electrolyte losses during exercise.

Heart and blood pressure: After running for a few months, your heart's walls thicken and the ventricles (internal chambers) increase in size. As a result more blood is sent to your lungs with each heartbeat, and your resting pulse can decline by 20 per cent or more.

If you run for 145 minutes per week, you are 40 per cent less likely than a sedentary person to have a heart attack. If you're overweight when you start running, then the resulting weight loss will lower your blood pressure, taking some of the strain off your heart.

Hormones: If you run above your lactate threshold pace (slightly slower than VO_2max) your body tends to produce more human-growth hormone, which boosts muscle building, accelerates fat breakdown, and speeds the repair of bones and connective tissues.

Running also seems to increase muscle cells' sensitivity to insulin, a key hormone released by the pancreas. In Type-I diabetics, this improved sensitivity can reduce insulin requirements; in Type-II diabetics, it decreases insulin resistance and promotes normal blood-glucose levels. Running also increases blood levels of a thyroid hormone called thyroxin, which increases protein synthesis, boosts mitochondria production (see Muscles) and encourages the breakdown of fat.

Joints: Running lubricates the joints to keep them supple and friction-free, but can lead to deterioration of the joint if disease or ageing of the joint is already present.

Lungs: Actually you can't improve the function of your lungs through training. They are already 'over-built' for even the most strenuous training, and fail to rush oxygen into your blood when you are working hard only because they are too 'stiff' to expand and bring in air at high enough rates. You can, however, improve the function of your respiratory muscles – the diaphragm and the muscles which run between your ribs – which makes breathing feel easier as you get fitter.

Muscles: Running increases the number of blood vessels which supply each muscle cell, raises the number of mitochondria inside cells (which enhances the cell's ability to use oxygen to produce energy), causes levels of aerobic enzymes within muscles to rise, and stimulates muscle cells to elevate their ability to burn fat for energy.

While running will not alter your own balance of fast-twitch and slow-twitch muscles fibre, endurance running can make fast-twitch cells more fatigue-resistant, i.e. more like slow-twitch fibres.

Resistance to disease and infection: If you run 15–30 miles per week you have a lower risk of infection than your sedentary neighbour. However, if you've just run a marathon, or are in heavy training, then your risk of infection actually goes up, because your immune system is not working at maximum efficiency as it recovers from the stresses of training or competition.

Running is the most natural exercise you can choose.

Respiratory system: Running causes the mucus within the sinuses and the Eustachian tube (which leads to the middle ear) to be dislodged – that's the coughing and spitting which normally accompany your first couple of miles. However, you should be aware of pollution – try to avoid running, if you can, during hours of peak traffic, don't jog at traffic lights, and run on the building side of the pavement. And running is more likely than other endurance sports to cause exercise-induced asthma. However, your running need not suffer if the condition is controlled medically.

Skin: Running improves your ability to sweat, tolerate heat and regulate body core temperature, and helps you withstand the cold in winter. It also improves conditions such as teenage acne, eczema and psoriasis.

3 Getting started

Someone once said that everything you need to know about running can be reduced to a single sentence: 'Put one foot in front of the other and repeat, remembering to alternate feet.'
While running is one of the most basic human activities, there are a few things you ought to think about before you dash out of your front door for your first run. To begin with, how fit are you? If you regularly participate in another physically demanding sport then you should be fine, as long as you don't try to break the 4-minute-mile barrier on your first day. Indeed, most people can safely embark on a graduated running programme without any further ado, but you should have a medical check-up first if you are overweight, have been seriously ill in the past 12 months, come from a family with a history of heart disease, or are over thirty-five years old. This is important: even if you feel fine now, you could have cardiac or other abnormalities which may cause trouble when you place your body under unaccustomed physical stress.

It's also useful to think about your goals. Those optimistic runners who throng the streets in the first few days of January every year, never to be seen in a pair of trainers again, usually make one of two common mistakes: either they set out with unrealistic expectations, or they go to the other extreme and don't set themselves any specific targets at all. In the first case, they become discouraged when they find they can't run 10 miles non-stop by the end of the first week: in the second, they lose interest because

they have no way of judging their progress.

This doesn't mean that you shouldn't set out with the long-term aim of completing a marathon (for example), or that it's wrong to run because you just want to feel fitter. What's important is to set yourself intermediate targets which will help to strengthen your resolve when the initial excitement wears off. The programme in this chapter (panel, p.11) is designed to lead to you to the point where you can comfortably run non-stop for half an hour. If that doesn't sound like much, bear in mind that in those 30 minutes you'll probably cover around 3 miles: if you can manage that, you're already fitter than over 50 per cent of the British population. Those New Year's resolution runners we mentioned earlier are generally kitted out in the latest high-tech running gear, but unless you really feel that making a heavy financial investment in the sport is the only thing that will keep you going, you don't need to bother with specialist clothing just yet. For the first week or two you can go out in pretty much anything, as long as it isn't too tight, too heavy or too warm. Lightweight trousers and a T-shirt or sweatshirt will be fine. But it is advisable to wear a proper pair of running shoes; a good sports shop will be able to recommend a pair for starting with. The main requirement is that your running shoes should have sufficient padding to absorb the shock of impact when your feet hit the ground – human legs weren't designed with Tarmac in mind.

The 10-week beginner's training programme

This schedule is designed to take you up to the point where you can comfortably run for 30 minutes without stopping or slowing to a walk. Each week, do the suggested run/walk routine (which should take about half an hour) four times, preferably alternating exercise days with rest days wherever possible: for example, you could train on Monday, Wednesday, Friday and Saturday.

Don't be afraid to go back and repeat a week if you're finding the programme hard going. Remember the story of the hare and the tortoise: at this stage, you definitely want to follow the tortoise's example.

Week 1
Run for 2 minutes, then walk for 4 minutes – do this five times.

Week 2
Run for 3 minutes, then walk for 3 minutes – do this five times.

Week 3
Run for 5 minutes, then walk for 2½ minutes – do this four times.

Week 4
Run for 7 minutes, then walk for 3 minutes – do this three times.

Week 5
Run for 8 minutes, then walk for 2 minutes – do this three times.

Week 6
Run for 9 minutes, then walk for 2 minutes – do this three times.

Week 7
Run for 9 minutes, then walk for 1 minute – do this three times.

Week 8
Run for 13 minutes, then walk for 2 minutes – do this twice.

Week 9
Run for 14 minutes, then walk for 1 minute – do this twice.

Week 10
Run for 30 minutes.

A good training run can create a marvellous sense of well-being.

So where are you going to take those all-important first steps? If you're at all bashful, the best place to start is either somewhere so quiet that no one will see you, or so busy that no one will notice you. Quiet locations are fairly easy to find if you live in the country; in built-up areas, school playing fields and other sports grounds are generally deserted early in the morning. You could also try a golf course, though you should stick to the edges unless you want to be chased by an irate groundsman in a motorised cart. As for busy locations, you can't beat your local park, which will usually be so full of other runners, people walking dogs and parents trying to placate crying children that nobody will take any notice of one extra jogger.

The surface you run on will also make a difference, but don't worry too much about that to begin with. Try to avoid hills for the moment, though. Hill running helps to build both muscular and cardiovascular strength, and it may well become a central feature of your training regime at a later stage, but right now, both uphills and downhills add new elements which will complicate your running. Our beginner's training programme is designed to take 10 weeks to get you to your target of running for 30 minutes consecutively. But like your mother always told you, don't try to run

Running surfaces

Many running injuries are caused or exacerbated by training on poor surfaces. The steeper the slope, the harder or more angled the surface, the greater the chances of an injury. Conversely, the best surfaces for running are firm, reasonably flat and provide some shock absorption. Here's a list of eight common running surfaces, ranked in order from most to least desirable:

1. Running track (cinder or tartan)
2. Soft mud path
3. Flat grass
4. Asphalt
5. Hard mud path
6. Concrete
7. Hard sand
8. Rough, potholed grass

If you have got access to a running track, it's a good place for beginners. It's flat and gentle on the legs, and you can judge exactly how far you've run. Stick to the outer lanes (unless you want to get screamed at by more experienced runners conducting timed sessions), and change direction every few laps; running in the same direction can place unnecessary strain on your joints and tendons, particularly if you're not used to running round bends.

Soft paths or grass are fine, provided of course that the surface is flat and even – turning an ankle in a concealed pothole will do nothing for your progress. If you do have to run on roads or pavements, asphalt is more forgiving than concrete.

Pavements are safer, though they can be uneven, and it's all too easy to catch a toe and go flying. If you train on the road (and in rural areas, you often have no choice), remember to run against the oncoming traffic, to give drivers more chance of seeing you and yourself more chance of diving into the ditch if they don't. Watch out too for roads with a pronounced camber, since running with one leg higher than the other for any length of time will increase your risk of injury. The same applies to beaches, which generally slant down towards the waterline, so change direction at frequent intervals and watch out for pebbles, shells, seaweed and anything else you might slip on.

The next time you pass a school playground during break time, stop and watch the children playing: see how they run naturally, without having to think about it. As adults, many of us lose this instinctive ability to run, and our first steps become awkward and self-conscious.

The proper position of the body during running is called 'form'. Of course, everyone is put together differently, so it's impossible to prescribe absolutely the way you should be running. Nevertheless, what follows are general principles of body mechanics which can be supplied to all runners. From time to time, it's worth examining the way you run (try looking at yourself in shop windows as you pass) and concentrating on eliminating any points of particularly bad form.

Posture

The most efficient way to run is with a posture that is erect, perpendicular to the ground. Your head, neck and shoulders should be lined up, not leaning forwards or backwards, and your upper body should be relaxed.

Motion

As you move, your arms, shoulders, hips and legs should all be pointing forward, and not swaying from side to side or leaning back. This is vital for efficient motion.

Arms

Keep your arms relaxed, swinging fairly low and close to your body. This way you don't need to expend much energy on them, because gravity will do most of the work for you. Ideally, your arms should simply follow the rhythm of your feet.

Legs

Sprinters run with a high knee lift because they need maximum stride length, leg speed and power. However, to maximise efficiency, other runners should stay lower on the ground and avoid a high back kick. Don't make the common mistake of lengthening your stride too far: stride *frequency*, not length, is the key to faster and more efficient running. The ideal is to bounce lightly and quickly off the ground, making your ankles do most of the work. You should feel a definite push in your calf muscles with every step; this means that they're taking some of the load away from the muscles of the upper leg.

Breathing

Maintaining an erect posture while running helps to maximise your ability to use your lung capacity. Apart from this, don't worry too much about breathing. Without even thinking, you will find yourself co-ordinating your breathing with your stride rate.

Stretching

If you do it properly, stretching is one of your most important weapons in the ongoing battle against injury: it helps to reduce the tension in your muscles, improves your blood circulation and makes you more flexible. If you don't stretch, there's a good chance you'll feel stiff and sore the day after a run.

If you're a sprinter, or any other kind of runner doing speedwork, you should stretch after you've warmed up. Otherwise, don't stretch before you run: when your muscles are cold, they're more easily strained. Instead, use the first few minutes of your run as a gentle warm-up, and stretch after you've finished, when the muscles are loose.

Ease into each stretch gently until you feel the muscle go taut. (If it hurts, you've gone too far.) Hold this position for 20 to 30 seconds, then slowly ease out again. Don't 'bounce' the stretch, as this can make the muscle sore.

The eight stretches that follow cater for the main muscles used in running. You can perform all eight after each run, or choose those which apply to the muscles which feel most in need of help. The shaded areas in the illustrations indicate where you should feel the stretch.

1. Upper calf

Stand two or three feet away from a wall and facing it. Keep your feet flat on the ground, lean forward and place your palms against the wall. Then lift your left heel off the ground by bending your left knee, keeping your right foot flat on the ground and your right knee, hip and back straight. Now lean forward by bending your elbows until you feel the stretch in your right calf. Repeat for the left calf.

2. Lower calf

Stand close enough to a wall that you can touch it with your palms without leaning. Lift your

left heel by bending the knee, keeping your right foot flat on the floor. Now bend your right knee and lower your body so that you feel the stretch near the bottom of your calf. Repeat for the left calf.

3. Iliotibial band

Stand at right angles to a wall, two or three feet away. Crossing your legs, lean towards the wall, supporting yourself with the palm of your right hand. Keeping your right knee and elbow straight, push your hips towards the wall until you feel the stretch down the outside of your left thigh. Repeat for the right leg.

4. Shins

Kneel down with your ankles and feet together and toes pointing behind you. Slowly sit down on your heels, pushing your ankles towards the floor and keeping them together, until you feel the stretch in your shins.

5. Groin

Sit on the floor with the soles of your feet together, your hands on your feet and your elbows resting against your knees or thighs. Push your knees towards the floor until you feel the stretch in your groin.

6. Buttock

Lie on your back with your left leg straight. Bend your right leg and bring it back towards the hip. Rotate your right heel towards your left hip and hold your right ankle with your left hand and your right knee with your right hand. Pull the leg evenly back towards your shoulders until you feel the stretch in your right buttock. Repeat for the left buttock.

7. Hamstring

Lie on your back with your left leg straight. Bend your right knee and bring it back towards your hip. With the knee still bent, grasp your

right hamstring. Then straighten the right leg until you feel the stretch in the hamstring. Repeat for the left hamstring.

8. Thigh

Lie on your stomach, with your left leg straight and your right bent at a 90-degree angle. Loop a rope or towel around your right ankle and hold onto both ends. Now raise the right leg off the ground, trying to straighten the knee against the tension of the rope or towel, until you feel the stretch in your thigh. Repeat for the left thigh.

before you can walk. We're not talking here about that hip-swivelling, arm-swinging race-walking you might have seen in the Olympics, just a relaxed stroll around the streets or the park. If you're a complete novice to running, go out walking for 20 minutes a day four days in a row, and then move up to 30 minutes for another four days. This will gradually prepare your legs for running, and it will also help you to get into a routine.

The next stage (i.e. Week 1 of the programme) is to start mixing a little running into your programme. Not a lot, just two minutes of running to every four of walking, repeating this until you've been on your feet for half an hour. The running in these early stages should be no more than a gentle jog, with your feet only just leaving the ground. If you find yourself getting out of breath, slow down to a walk until you're ready to try jogging again. A good way to judge your pace is the 'talk test': you should be able to carry on a conversation while you run without feeling unduly uncomfortable. There'll be plenty of time to zip along at speeds that leave you gasping for breath when you're a bit fitter.

Don't worry about how far you're running. One of the biggest mistakes beginners make is to get obsessed with distance, adding an extra mile to their routine every few days. Most of them aren't ready for that, and a drastic progression like this is often a shortcut to early burn-out. Remember, think in terms of minutes on your feet, not miles covered.

The 10-week programme involves running four times a week: *don't* get impatient and start filling in the gaps. The fundamental principle of physical training is that the body adapts to increased stress levels by getting stronger. Thus, if you increase the effort you put into your running a little and then give

your body time to adjust, you'll find that the same speed feels easier the next time you try it. However, if you increase the effort too quickly and don't give your body time to make the adjustment, you'll just become more and more tired. This is because the strengthening and rebuilding take place while the body is at rest. In other words, the improvement in your fitness is actually going on, paradoxically, when you're doing nothing. Hence the rest days.

Once you start the programme, do your best to stick to it. It's a good idea to make a chart that sets out what you're supposed to do each day, and then tick it off as you do it. At the same time, don't stick to the plan at all costs if common sense dictates otherwise. If you feel any kind of strain in your feet, calves, ankles or knees, stick to walking or have an extra day's rest. Similarly, if you get to the end of a week and find that the scheduled exercise is tougher than you'd like, don't be afraid to go back and repeat that week. The important thing is to move up through the programme steadily and without injury.

If you suspect that you're going to have difficulty motivating yourself to stick at your new running programme, take steps in advance to make it harder to give up. One way to do this is to find a training partner: either an experienced runner who knows what you're going through and can advise and encourage accordingly, or a fellow novice who can go through it with you. It's harder to give up if someone else is involved, and just having someone to talk to can help to take your mind off the running itself when the going gets tough.

It's also a good idea to fix a regular time of day for your running routine. If you're a 'morning person', by all means go out early, before work. The streets and other public places are relatively empty at

No one is immortal, but we all have a choice to make: are we going to sit back and accept the physical deterioration that comes from neglecting our bodies, or are we going to do everything in our power to improve our quality – and length – of life? For scientific evidence suggests that regular exercise helps to stave off the most common degenerative diseases such as diabetes, kidney failure and heart disease. Just as importantly, the positive mental attitude that an exercise programme stimulates is a great weapon against the temptation to fade away into old age.

Of course, the ageing process cannot be denied. As we grow older, our body's cells lose their power to renew themselves, which means that some tissues start to perform less efficiently. We lose elasticity, and there is a decline in our maximum heart rate and in the maximum power output of our muscles.

Even so, it is possible to maintain flexibility and strength through conscientious training. Look at the examples of Linford Christie and Merlene Ottey, Irishman Eamonn Coghlan, Joyce Smith and Priscilla Welch. New Zealander Jack Foster ran 2:11 at the age of forty-one – having only taken up running when he was thirty-three! Indeed, people who only take up running at a relatively advanced age, or who return to the sport after a long break, often make astonishing progress which can be put down to the surge of enthusiasm they experience when they discover what they're capable of. They can continue to get better for several years, as the improvement due to training outweighs the decline due to ageing. In general, though, research shows that after the age of thirty-five, your strength and speed will decline by around half of one per cent per year.

If you want to start running when you're in your forties or older, all the advice in this chapter applies to you, but with a few extra provisos. Above all, remember that older runners get hurt more easily and heal more slowly than younger ones. This makes it all the more important not to push yourself too hard, too quickly. When you're running, try to become aware of the line between comfort and discomfort: if you never cross that line, you won't improve, but if you cross it too far or too often, injury and subsequent discouragement will beckon.

You must also give your body plenty of time to recover between exertions, especially in the early days. Even the fittest and keenest older runners have discovered that their bodies work best if they limit themselves to three runs a week, and you should too. If you're desperate to fill in some of the gaps, try some gentle swimming, cycling or some other cross-training activity (see Chapter 13). But remember, your body is supposed to be recovering, so don't push yourself too hard.

If you do reach the stage where you want to test yourself in a race, age will be no barrier. Quite the reverse, in fact. As the people who took up jogging in the 'running boom' of the 1970s have aged, so the balance of the British running world has altered. Organised Veterans' races (a Veteran, in British running terms, is simply any woman over thirty-five or man over forty – in the USA they're known by the more grandiose term 'Masters') take place all over the country at every distance, and most road races have special-category prizes for Vets, even though, on the female side in particular, the winning Veteran is often the overall champion anyway. For competitive purposes, Veterans are generally divided into five-year age bands: M40 (men aged forty to forty-four), M45 (forty-five to fifty), and so on. Newcomers to the sport are sometimes surprised by the number of these bands, and if you need convincing that running isn't just a young person's sport, go to a major road race and look out for the M70s. If they can keep running into their seventies, why shouldn't you have a go in your forties or fifties?

this time of day, which is a bonus if you're at all embarrassed about being watched. The down side is that your body is less flexible in the morning, so you need to be extra careful not to overdo it. Alternatively, you can go running during your lunch break (though if your place of work doesn't have showers, this might be a little unpleasant for you and your colleagues afterwards!) or as soon as you get home from work. Some people prefer to wait until after dark, when the streets are deserted; however, if you leave it too late you might find it hard to sleep, as your body will still be too 'awake' from its exertions.

Once you start running regularly, and especially in warm weather, it's time to start thinking about what you wear to run in. You'll need some running shorts (in summer) or tights (in winter), and a lightweight, showerproof anorak or running top if you intend to go training in bad weather. Wear this over a T-shirt – if you wear a sweatshirt as well, you'll be too hot after just a few minutes' running. In hot weather, you might find a running vest preferable to a T-shirt.

You should also buy yourself some proper running shoes at this stage, as even the most comfortable aerobics or tennis shoes won't give you the support you need once you start running any distance. See Chapter 4 for more on what to look for when buying shoes.

When you've successfully completed the 10-week programme, give yourself a pat on the back – you're a runner! So what do you do now? Much depends on the reasons why you decided to take up running. If your goal is simply to improve your fitness, then the world is your oyster. You can experiment with different terrains, try running a little further or a little faster – with the emphasis on 'a little'. Listen to your body and react accordingly. If what you're doing feels too

easy, try pushing yourself a bit harder: if you're struggling, ease back or take an extra day's rest between runs. Chapter 5 contains detailed information on different kinds of training; experiment with these and find what works for you.

If your aim is to lose weight, then you should gradually increase the amount of running you do each week. Don't worry about running faster, but bear in mind that your body doesn't start burning fat until you've been exercising for about half an hour. Other forms of aerobic exercise such as swimming, cycling and rowing are also good fat-burning activities, and you can add these to your programme for variety, if you like.

The key to weight loss is simple: you need to use up more fuel through exercise than you are taking in through eating. Thus, if you run more and eat less, you should lose weight. However, *what* you eat is also important. To avoid damaging your health, try to alter your diet so that it contains the same nutrients but fewer calories. Above all, cut out foods which are high in fat and sugar, as they tend to have lots of calories and little nutritional value.

If you find at the end of your beginner's programme that you need another specific goal to keep you running, then why not enter a race? The possibilities here are almost endless. There are track races over every distance from 100 to 10,000 metres: road races (which don't always take place exclusively on roads) at a variety of distances, most commonly 5 and 10 kilometres, 5 and 10 miles and the half-marathon; the marathon (26 miles, 385 yards), seen by many as the ultimate running challenge; 'ultra' events over any distance from 30 miles to infinity (well, almost); cross-country races in the winter; fell races in mountainous areas; multi-sport events such as triathlons and duathlons, which combine running with swimming, cycling and other disciplines; and all manner of novelty events.

For your first race, though, set your sights fairly low. Many road races are accompanied by a 'fun run' over two or three miles, and these are ideal for your first competitive effort. Local papers usually advertise any events that are coming up, and *Runner's World* carries comprehensive listings of races of all kinds. To get the most out of your first race, try to find one with a fairly flat course, and aim for a congenial time of year; spring and autumn, when the weather is likely to be fine but not too humid, are popular with road racers. If you have a training partner, get them to run the race with you, and try to persuade your friends and family to come and cheer you on.

Don't succumb to the temptation to start too fast. Even if the entire field is out of sight a couple of minutes after the gun (and in a fun run, that's not very likely), stick to a tempo you're comfortable with. Don't worry about winning, or even about overtaking other runners – the chances are that a nine-year-old will streak past you at some point, but that doesn't matter. Just relax and settle into your usual training pace. If you feel good at the end, you can always put on a heroic sprint for the finish line which will impress the hell out of the spectators. After all, this is the time to show off: you said you were going to take up running, and now you've done it. Feels good, doesn't it?

Dressed for success

Running is unusual. It is a sport awash with equipment, gadgets and products intended to make you a healthier, happier, safer, more comfortable and, by implication, better athlete. Yet very little of it can be regarded as truly essential. It isn't.

The one exception is shoes. You can make do with an old pair of shorts, a gash T-shirt and a pair of black work socks, but poor or inappropriate shoes will soon take a toll. That applies as much to the complete novice as to the experienced club runner. That's the reason the majority of this chapter is devoted to

shoes and why most of your time and money spent on running equipment should equally be devoted to shoes.

The single biggest problem most people have is actually finding a pair of shoes they like, or more precisely, a pair their body likes. The process is complicated by the dozen or more brands, the hundreds of models and the proliferation of technology in the market. What you should first remember is that no shoe is perfect for everyone. Far from it: feet are

A pair of the right shoes is all a runner truly needs.

like fingerprints; no two pairs are identical and, while many will fit into a few broad categories, you should pay more attention to your own needs than those of a friend or clubmate.

Broadly speaking, there are shoes that are suitable for you and the role you intend to put them to and there are ones that are not. If you are expecting a pair that will make you a markedly better runner, you are dreaming. Shoes that you can forget about while you run, don't let you down and allow you to train and race injury-free are about as much as you can realistically expect. Looking at it from the negative side, a poor or inappropriate pair of shoes will hurt your running.

For those who are dipping a toe into the waters of the running-shoe market for the first time, here's a basic guide to how you should proceed if you're training on the roads.

1. Don't skimp – buy a good running shoe

This is the single most important piece of advice you can receive and it applies as much to the beginner as to the experienced runner. Only a good shoe will give you enough shock absorption, motion control, flexibility and durability.

You may only be running a few miles to start with, once or twice a week, but resist the temptation to go out in a pair of football trainers or tennis shoes. The risk of injury is too great as is the danger of muscle or joint soreness and pain that can only be prevented by decent running-specific footwear.

If you are wondering how to find a good running shoe, begin with the price. Technical running shoes start at about £40. Be suspicious of anything cheaper. More money usually means greater durability, more technical features and greater quality. Pay the money. It's worth it. Your shoes are the only critical

purchase you have to make. A good pair of running shoes should last on average between 500–600 miles, although the manufacturers consider anything that happens after 300 miles to be fair wear and tear.

2. Understand pronation

Running is a complex biomechanical process in which you strike the ground first on the outside of your heel. Then your foot rolls downwards and inwards as it hits the ground. Finally, the heel lifts from the ground and you push off from the ball of your foot to move forwards. The rotation of the foot inwards and downwards as it hits the ground is called pronation. It is a completely natural process. In fact, if you don't pronate you can't walk. Pronation is a good thing in that it helps the foot absorb the shock of impact.

Problems occur with runners who *overpronate*. The initial phase of the gait is the same but their feet roll too far inwards. This is a common problem that can lead to injuries, particularly in the lower leg and knee. Some runners suffer from the opposite problem – that is, they *underpronate* and their feet roll inwards only a little after contact. Their feet are said to be rigid and don't absorb shock very well. This can similarly lead to injury.

3. Understand your foot type

Most runners will be able to determine whether they have a normal, underpronating or overpronating foot from looking at their arch. The arch determines how your feet and legs will function when you run.

Flat feet usually overpronate. High-arched feet are more prone to underpronate. And if you have normal arches then you probably also have a normal gait. Studies suggest that the

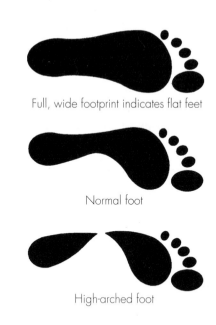

Full, wide footprint indicates flat feet

Normal foot

High-arched foot

The wet test helps you analyse your arch.

Ordinarily, running shoes come in three basic shapes – straight, semi-curved and curved – which match the three types of footprints isolated in the wet test. As a general rule, overpronators should wear a shoe built on a straight last. Those with a normal gait need to look for a semi-curved last and underpronators need shoes which are more curved. There are also a few other characteristics to consider.

If you have flat feet and overpronate you need a shoe that will prevent your foot rolling in too far, i.e. a motion-control shoe. Many motion-control shoes have a straight shape that gives maximum support to your foot. Other characteristics to look for are a firm rather than soft midsole, a two-density midsole with the firmer material on the inside of the shoe to prevent excessive pronation and a firm heel counter to minimise rearfoot motion.

If you have high-arched feet and underpronate, your feet won't absorb shock very well, so you need a cushioned shoe. Also you should look for a shoe that allows you to roll inwards, since this helps to absorb shock. Avoid any shoes with a medial post. Cushioned shoes tend to be less supportive and work with the foot rather than trying to control it. You need a shoe with a soft cushioned midsole and a curved or semi-curved shape that permits foot motion as you run.

If you have normal arches and pronate normally then you are lucky. You fall into the widest group and will therefore have the widest choice of shoes. You won't need to search for any special features. Focus on the fit and comfort of the shoes rather than any features that control motion or absorb shock. Your ideal shoes should have a slightly curved shape and don't control foot motion as motion-control shoes do.

division between normal, high-arched and flat feet is approximately 50-25-25. If you are uncertain which group you fall into, the easiest way to analyse your arch is with the wet test. After taking a bath or shower look at the shape your wet foot makes on the floor. A full wide footprint is a sign of a low arch and a flat foot. A print that shows the complete foot with a moderate curve round the centre suggests a normal foot, while a print that is largely a heel and forefoot without a centre is almost certainly high-arched.

4. Matching foot type to shoe type

Once you have discovered how much you pronate, you have the basic information for determining the characteristics you should look for in a shoe. A key factor is the shape of the last the shoe was made on. Usually you can see the shape of the shoe by looking at its outsole.

5. Use a specialist retailer

Even if you have followed all the previous steps and understood them, it is still advisable to go to a specialist running shop to buy your shoes. If you are in any doubt, the salespeople, who are usually experienced runners, will be able to tell you if you show signs of needing any special features in your shoes. You should be able to find a specialist by looking in the *Yellow Pages* or in the back of a running magazine like *Runner's World*.

Here are some other points you need to remember when buying a new pair of shoes: shop in the late afternoon when your feet are at their largest; they swell when you run, so you need to duplicate this. Wear the socks you'll wear when you run; if you don't have any, buy some before buying the shoes. Make sure the salesperson measures both of your feet. Most of us have one foot bigger than the other and you should obviously be fitted for the larger foot.

6. Make sure your shoe fits

This might seem obvious, but it's surprising how often people walk out of a shop with a doubt about the fit. This is the most important factor in choosing a pair of shoes. If it fits correctly then you are a long way down the road to finding

---

Before you try on any shoes the salesperson should talk to you about your running to help guide you to particular pairs of shoes. Here are five questions they should ask you. Be suspicious of the shoe and its standards if they don't ask at least a variation of these:

1. How long have you been running?
2. How much mileage are you doing?
3. Where do you do most of your running?
4. How much do you weigh?
5. Are you aware of any foot problems, such as flat or underpronating feet?

---

that perfect pair of shoes. A running shoe that fits should be snug but not too tight. One common mistake is buying shoes that are too small. You may actually have to buy shoes that are a half or a full size too big. The following guidelines should help you determine whether the shoes really do fit you properly:

▶ Check that there is enough room in the top by pressing down with your thumb just above the longest toe. The thumb should fit between the end of the shoe and your toe.

▶ Check the width. Your foot shouldn't be tight, neither should it slide around in the shoe.

▶ Your heel should fit snugly into the rear of the shoe and it should not slide up and down as you walk or run.

▶ Take the shoes for a test run. Or at least run around the shop in them. You may feel slightly ridiculous, but not as stupid as walking out of the shop with a pair that are fine for walking but not for running.

▶ Try a number of different models. The fit and feel of the shoes will vary between manufacturers, as each makes its shoes on a different last.

7. Stick with a winner

When you've found a shoe you like, stick with it. Ignore the new models and technology that inevitably will come onto the market. Remember, if you have discovered a shoe you can run in without trouble or thought then you have the perfect shoe. Don't dabble with that winning formula.

The view from a shoe

Running shoes were once no more than a piece of canvas stuck on top of a solid slab of rubber. Things have changed. Today's running shoes are high-tech pieces of equipment which use state-of-

Extending the life of your shoes

► The best way to clean your shoes is with a bowl of clean water, soap and a soft bristled brush. Sticking them in the washing machine is tempting but generally to be avoided. Detergents can create chemical reactions with the materials and cements used within the shoe that can cause the shoes to break down quicker than expected. If you must toss your shoes into a washing machine, only use warm water and no detergents.

► For all the visible mess on the outside, the part of the shoe that often needs the most attention is the inside. After a few weeks of running in them, the shoes

can develop a noxious odour. The best way to remove it is with a deodorant from the chemist or by brushing the insides with a little baking soda. Washing the insoles regularly also helps and keeping the shoes dry after running in them will also help.

► It is not a bad idea to own two pairs of shoes, particularly in winter when your shoes are constantly wet after a run. If you buy two pairs of a similar design, you can lessen your chances of an overuse injury by slightly changing the gait pattern.

► Be careful about re-soling your shoes to extend their

life. The midsole is often the first part of the shoe to give out and, as it cannot be replaced, putting on a new outsole alone will serve no useful purpose.

► The best way to keep your shoes in the best possible shape for running is to use them only for running. Running is a simple but specialised sport; its demands are duplicated in part in other sports but always in combination with other movements. Those other movements, particularly in tennis, football or basketball, will tear your running shoes apart.

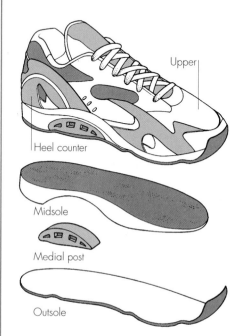

Upper

Heel counter

Midsole

Medial post

Outsole

the-art materials to protect your body from the mile after mile of pavement pounding. As the shoes have become more complicated, so too have the terminologies used to describe them. The diagram alongside gives a rough guide to the sections of a shoe and an explanation of their role.

Upper: The part of the shoe that wraps round and over the top of the foot. Usually it is constructed from a combination of breathable mesh and synthetic leather.

Heel counter: A firm piece of reinforced plastic that surrounds the heel to control rearfoot motion. It can either be encased in the upper or on the outside.

Midsole: The technical heart of the shoe. This is the cushioning layer between the upper and the outsole. It is usually made from EVA (a soft foam), Polyurethane (a synthetic rubber), or a combination of the two. Two-density midsoles have a firmer piece of material on the inside of the shoe. This helps to limit pronation. The midsole is also the area where the manufacturers add their primary technologies – cushioning materials such as air, gel or high-tech plastics.

Medial post: A firm material or device inserted into the inside of the midsole (over the arch) that is designed to limit pronation.

Outsole: The section of the shoe that comes into contact with the ground. This is generally made from various combinations of rubber.

Specialist footwear

Trail shoes

These are a fairly recent addition to the running-shoe market, intended for training on a variety of off-road surfaces like dirt, grass or rocky trails. They are close cousins to road models, with the same kind of midsole and rearfoot control you would expect for running on tarmac. In fact, as many are adapted versions of road designs, they are equally effective on- and off-road. The important differences are in the outsole, which is usually a thicker studded or waffled rubber design for grip and durability, and in the upper which is again tougher, more durable and often water-resistant. If you train regularly off-road, you should consider a trail shoe. Your everyday road shoe, as well as struggling to cope with the conditions, will also deteriorate much more quickly when put through demanding runs on the trails.

Racing shoes

Racing flats are the minimalist end of the road market. Major elements of the design of the shoe are sacrificed to achieve one goal – reduced weight. The result is a shoe built on a curved last with a thin EVA midsole, blown rubber outsole and predominantly mesh upper. Such a shoe could help skim 30 seconds off a 10K time and as much as two minutes from a marathon best. But be warned, as there are just about no cushioning and stability features, you could be doing yourself some serious harm if you are not suited to racers. Anyone who has any kind of stability problems, is heavy (over 11 stone) or cannot run a marathon inside 3.10, or a half-marathon inside 1:40, should avoid them. That is not to say that you cannot gain the benefit of a lighter shoe, just that you should avoid the under-270gram shoes at the featherweight end of the market. Even within the racing-flat market there are grades of lightness from those under 160g intended for races of 10K and below to the more substantial marathon racers which are closer to 250g. Again the lighter the shoe, the fewer the features and the quicker it will wear.

Fell shoes

The demands of training and racing on the mountain fells of Northern England, Scotland and Wales require a shoe which is as tough and rugged as the competitors themselves. There are two key design elements – the grip of the sole and the durability of the upper. Look for a thick studded carbon rubber design on the outsole with full studs on the whole, particularly the edges, of the sole with a toe wrap. The upper should be a tough, synthetic material that either keeps water out or dries quickly. Fell runners don't need a great deal of cushioning because of the terrain – in any case, a thick midsole would make the shoe unstable. Fell shoes can be worn for cross-country races.

Cross-country spikes

Like fell models, cross-country spikes are low-profile shoes, with a tough synthetic upper and a front spike plate that provides the grip for the mud, grass and streams of the country. The length of spike you choose should depend on the conditions, but 15mm should be the maximum; usually shorter lengths will do. Longer spikes tend to pick up more rubbish and leaves than shorter ones. In particularly boggy conditions you can tape around the spike to provide more grip. Lubricating them with vaseline also keeps water out of the plate and makes them easier to remove.

Track spikes

Track spikes come in two varieties, those for sprinting and those for middle and long distance. The difference is in the weight and the cushioning. Sprinters basically demand nothing more than a spike plate stuck to the bottom of a skeleton upper, which is essentially all they have. Middle and long-distance runners equally demand a shoe that will provide traction on the tartan track but combined with some rearfoot control and a wedge of EVA under the heel. Built on a curved last, they are still frighteningly light. A word of warning, try to train sparingly in spikes. Distance runners often feel soreness on the calf and Achilles after a track session in spikes.

Kit and clothing

Although shoes are the only essential piece of equipment for running, there is no shortage of kit specifically designed for the rest of the body.

The cotton T-shirt is still the most common piece of training equipment. It's basic, cheap and functional. But on a warm day when you start to sweat heavily, the cotton will tend to hold the moisture, become heavier and, as the moisture cools, put a chill on your body. T-shirts made from technical fabrics like Coolmax or Tactel, which are lighter than cotton, are better at 'wicking' sweat away from your body. You stay dry and so does your shirt. Alternatively, wear a singlet, which is often made from the same technical materials but also provides a cut which allows air to circulate more freely around your body.

Shorts are less important and again it's all basically about comfort. Try to avoid any with rough seams, over-tight elastic or an awkward cut that can rub and chafe. Check the waistband too; thicker ones tend to be more comfortable. Women's designs, which are much rarer, have higher waistbands, a more generous cut around the hips and are longer in the leg.

Socks have surprisingly also joined the technical-clothing revolution. Cotton ones tend to have the same problems as cotton T-shirts, with the added irritation of causing blisters. More technical models offer materials which again wick moisture away from the skin or come in a double-layer design (two socks sewn together) to reduce the friction which often leads to blisters.

The power of layering

There was a time when almost everyone who ventured outside in the winter thought that wearing one good layer of clothing was the best way to stay warm and protected against the cold, wind and snow.

Run just a few miles in that big, heavyweight fleecy sweatshirt and it won't be long before you are uncomfortably wet and chilled to the bone. The secret of maximum comfort during your winter run is layering. This doesn't mean one thick layer, but two or three lightweight ones. Such a system allows perspiration to escape more readily while holding in more heat, thus keeping you warmer and drier. If you become overheated during a run, simply remove a layer – you can always put it back on again if you feel the chill.

Layering works because moisture moves more easily through a couple of thin layers than one thick one. If you wear the right fabrics, perspiration is wicked away from your skin by the first layer, then evaporates or is picked up by the next layer. The trick is to wear the appropriate clothing and layer the pieces properly. Indeed, wear one wrong item and the system won't work. A good layering system for a runner uses at most three layers on the upper body. Add another and it will be too bulky and uncomfortable for running.

The first layer should wick moisture off your skin and move it to the outside, to protect you from chilling. It should be lightweight and fit snugly. It's important to wear synthetic wicking materials rather than absorbent fabrics (such as cotton), which get wet and stay wet.

The middle layer should be there to insulate further by creating additional air space. You should only need a middle layer in very cold conditions. Although this layer might be a bit heavier than the first, it must still wick moisture outward, away from the skin. It should fit loosely over the first layer and should be easy to remove, so that you can adjust for weather conditions.

The outer layer is the protective shell which shelters you from the wind, rain or cold, while also allowing perspiration to evaporate. It should be large enough to fit loosely over the other layers. If the insulation layer is compressed by a tight layer, your system will lose efficiency. Ventilation is also important, as this allows the other layers to perform better.

Well-planned layering will keep you warm and dry.

Safety kit

Winter running, especially in poorly lit rural regions, can be a dangerous business. The only way to make it safer is to ensure you are visible. Most manufacturers have realised this and now incorporate reflective trim on their shoes and add it to all items of winter clothing. To be on the safe side you should consider wearing a special reflective bib which can be easily picked out by a car's headlights, together with a small flashing light that you can clip somewhere on your back or waist. You will be able to see traffic coming towards you but not from behind.

Additional items

The urge to time and compare is too great for many runners to last long without a watch. At the basic level you will need a digital stopwatch that records elapsed time. From there you can move on to one with a lap counter, which will take your splits (a 30-lap memory is about the most you will need), a countdown timer for short interval sessions and a recovery timer. Try to find a watch with buttons on the front of the watch which are easier to press while on the run.

During the summer months, sunglasses have become all the vogue in running and triathlon circles. Models that come in a variety of shades, protect against UV-A and UV-B and stay rooted to your head even under extreme conditions are now commonplace.

Carrying water in the summer months is something which has also spawned a number of product solutions. At the professional end there are special backpacks, fitted with bladders and tubes to sip through while you run, while at the lower end there are shaped, easy-grip

The extras are up to you ...

drinking bottles and various systems for carrying water bottles around your waist. All have their supporters and detractors.

5 Different types of training

The great ultra-distance runner, Arthur Newton, is credited with the saying: 'Train first for distance, then for speed'. And certainly, being able to run for about an hour non-stop should be the first priority for those new to running. But after that, assuming that you don't want to follow in Newton's footsteps and compete in the 56-mile Comrades Marathon in South Africa, you'll need to think about introducing some variety into your training if you want to improve, no matter what your goals in running are. Coaches and athletes are constantly experimenting with techniques and training methods to improve performance, but there are some tried and tested principles and training aids outlined below that you may want to consider.

Fartlek

Fartlek is a Swedish term meaning 'speedplay', literally playing with your speed during training. It's done without a watch, but rather according to a rhythm that is not pre-determined. For example, you may choose to train on a golf course and vary your speed, from gentle jogging to all-out sprinting, according to which hole you're on. Or, in town, you can try quickening your pace when a bus passes you, maintaining that speed until passed by another, at which point you slow down. In this way, you have no way of knowing how long each session will be. Speedplay usefully mimics the demands of a race, when the decision to surge or break away from the pack may be taken by another runner.

Hills

Hill training can be beneficial whether your aim is actually to compete over undulating terrain, or simply as a means of improving overall fitness and leg strength.

Hill training forces your body to work harder, and your leg muscles to contract more powerfully than normal because they must overcome gravity to move you upwards. Research has shown that hill training will increase the concentration of 'aerobic enzymes' in your leg muscles – the chemicals which allow muscles to function at high levels for long periods without tiring.

For best results you need to find a short, sharp hill of at least 25 metres, and a hilly course (sand dunes, countryside) where you can run up and down almost continuously for at least 30 minutes, and to try and incorporate one hill session into your training per week.

The short hill session is brutal but brief: after a jog warm-up of 10 minutes, run up the hill at faster than 10-kilometre pace, and recover by jogging back down. Surge up again when you feel you're ready, and aim for four or five repetitions at first. Increase difficulty by adding reps, or cutting down on recovery time.

The longer hill session requires nothing more than to attack the rolling terrain for 30 minutes at a pace slightly slower than 10-kilometre race pace.

Improving VO₂max

Your body uses more oxygen as the intensity of exercise increases, and, at a point shortly before you reach maximum capacity, or speed, the rate of oxygen consumption reaches a plateau and does not increase further. That point is where you have reached maximum oxygen consumption. Typically that point is at around 3-kilometre race pace – your heart is sending as much oxygen as it can to your muscles. If you run faster than 3-kilometre pace, energy is supplied anaerobically, i.e. without oxygen.

Increases in mileage and increases in intensity of training can both improve VO_2max levels. However, research has shown very little uplift in runners running over 70 miles per week, whereas a reduction in overall mileage with a corresponding increase in training intensity has proven a surer way to

Hill training is concentrated running at its best.

increase the level of VO_2max.

Quite simply, faster training puts more pressure on the heart and muscles to improve, in particularly your IIa muscle fibres. These cells help you to run explosively but normally are bad at using oxygen. Faster training helps them to 'learn' how to use oxygen more efficiently.

How fast should you train? Between 90 and 100 per cent of your VO_2max is best, which equates to equal or faster than your 10K race speed, up to but no faster than your 3-kilometre pace.

And how often? No more than two sessions per week at between 90–100 per cent or you will overtrain. For your other sessions, train more moderately.

Fast-paced running gradually enables your body to take in more oxygen.

Interval training and repetitions

Interval training is a more structured version of fartlek, usually done on the track, alternating effort with recovery, although the possibilities are endless – Hungarian coach Mihaly Igloi was said to have 40,000 interval workouts! Nevertheless the basic elements to be arranged remain constant: the distance of the fast run; the recovery or interval between the efforts; how many repetitions of the effort; the speed of the efforts; the activity during the intervals, i.e., complete rest, jogging or walking. If done on the track, exact comparisons can be made between sessions.

The priority is to keep the time of the

efforts as even as possible, rather than to run each effort flat out, which would be impossible, as lactic acid accumulation would bring you to a stop fairly quickly. You will need to try out a variety of speeds on the track, especially if you are used to running longer intervals, or 'repetitions', on the road.

A good sample session for beginners is: 6–8 x 4000 metres, with 90 seconds to 3 minutes' recovery (walk or jog). Your speed should be somewhere between your 10-kilometre and 5-kilometre race pace.

A repetition or 'reps' training session is ideal if you're looking to increase your running speed, and to measure your increase in fitness. Generally an interval session becomes a reps session when the distance run increases to over 1,000 or 1,200 metres, but there is no set distance for either.

Choose a set course of between 1 and 2 miles, run it a set number of times at a fast pace, and include a fixed period of rest in between each run. For example, you might run a 1.5-mile loop six times with three minutes' recovery between each effort.

Try to find a course which you can use year-round – quiet roads (well lit if possible) are ideal. The same course enables you to measure your improvement, and the distance is an ideal guide to your fitness and your body's ability to take up and use oxygen.

Lactate threshold and threshold training

As you run faster than roughly 15-kilometre race pace, lactate begins to accumulate in the blood which eventually will be at such a level that no more oxygen can be delivered to your working muscles. Lactate threshold speed (LTS) is the running speed above which there is a sudden increase in the lactate level in your blood.

Raising your lactate threshold level enables you to hold off this increase and will allow you to race faster over 5 kilometres and 10 kilometres, and indeed longer distances. For most runners LTS is closely related to race pace: 5K pace is about 5–6 per cent faster than LTS; 10K pace about 2–3 per cent quicker. LTS is about 2–3 per cent faster than half-marathon pace, and 5–6 per cent faster than marathon pace. A session which helps lower lactate production is a 'tempo' run – a session where you run for 20–30 minutes at a pace about 12–15 seconds per mile slower than your 10-kilometre race pace. This pace corresponds almost exactly with LTS and helps the muscles and cardiovascular system to adapt so that less lactic acid is produced.

The long run

The long run forms the cornerstone of almost every training schedule for runners regularly competing in half-marathons and above. It is the long run which is often seen as the key component for a beginner looking to complete a first marathon, and is the staple club run up and down the country.

But does scientific evidence back up the anectodal? Yes and no. There is no doubt that the long run teaches your body to burn fat and spare glycogen for the marathon distance, as well as stimulating capillary development – leading to more efficient oxygen transport to the working muscles. Long runs also activate your fast-twitch muscle cells – the ones responsible for speed and power – because your slow-twitch fibres begin to tire after about 45 minutes. As a result, the aerobic potential of your fast-twitch fibres increases, which benefits your endurance. Crucially also, the long run gives you the psychological ability to cope with long distances.

However, running long distances regularly in training damages your body by breaking down muscle fibres, depleting muscle glygocen, and allowing waste products to accumulate. Research also shows that it is intensity, not duration, which will make you a more effective runner, even at longer distances. Thus, running 8 miles at your marathon pace in training will prepare you better for your 26.2-mile race effort than 16 miles run at a pace considerably slower than your target race pace.

Research suggests that merely plodding along at a slow pace teaches you above all to plod along at a slow pace – long, slow distance making you a long, slow distance runner.

However, the answer is simple: you need merely to inject about 20 seconds of faster running every few minutes, bursts which activate your fast-twitch fibres perfectly, but which are too short to induce any lactic acid build-up which will unduly tire you.

Another session involves running the middle portion of your run at marathon pace, teaching your body to handle and recognise your target speed; for example, five miles at moderate speed, five miles at marathon pace, then five miles easy pace.

Peaking

If you compete at any level, your race performances will improve if you are properly prepared – and that means adequately rested as well as adequately trained. Obviously the amount you need to taper before a race depends on the importance of that race to you. But the chances are that, no matter how important, you will not have rested enough.

Top runners plan their competitive year well in advance, usually with one or two major goals. For most of us, however, the year is made up of training and racing, and the two often conflict. You may, for example, be in training for a marathon, but also be needed by your club to complete in a 10K.

Using shorter distance races is actually a good way, research reveals, to prepare for the long distance. Running a 5 kilometres, for example, some weeks before your target 10 kilometres, gets you used to a more uncomfortable intensity, but can also provide accurate advance information on how you'll do in the longer race, as long as conditions are similar.

Running a 10 kilometres before a marathon is fine, as long as you realise you won't be in the best-rested shape for the shorter distance. Even in the midst of marathon training, though, you can do yourself justice over 10 kilometres if you taper correctly, and that means four days of minimal – but brisk – running in the week before the event. For example, for a Sunday 10-kilometre, run a mile warm-up followed by 4 x 400m at 10-kilometre speed (with equal recoveries) on the Monday before, 3 x 400m on the Tuesday, two on the Wednesday, and one on the Thursday (all with the mile warm-up and recoveries), then nothing further until the race.

Your marathon training will not suffer; indeed it will benefit from the pace injection of a fast 10 kilometres.

Before the marathon, do not run a race of over half-marathon distance for at least three weeks before the event, otherwise your leg muscles simply won't have recovered in time.

Resistance training

Perhaps the earliest recorded example of resistance training was the Greek athlete Milo who, in the sixth century BC, lifted a growing heifer each day until it was four years old. As the weight of the heifer increased, so did Milo's ability and strength.

The same principle applies to a number of running devices and techniques which, by making running more difficult, enable you to increase strength and arguably fitness.

Resistance in any form will make you run more slowly, but extra weight by wearing a weighted vest or carrying dumb-bells, for example, will force you to work much harder. However, extra weight can alter your running form, and make you run in an 'unnatural' way.

Adding resistance to all your runs will simply make you a slower runner; however, some sessions may benefit: for example, short intervals, where you are trying to run faster than normal anyway, or hill sessions, where resistance would rapidly increase leg power.

Training on different terrain, i.e. sand or mud, also makes normal running more difficult. Both will stretch your Achilles tendons and calf muscles and both help you burn significantly more calories during a run (jogging on loose sand burns about 20 per cent more calories per mile than running on firm ground).

However, different terrain will also lead to muscle soreness, and, again, will make you run more slowly. The answer? Use resistance training no more than twice a week, and make sure that during the sessions your pace does not decline too much. If at all, use resistance as other intensity sessions like intervals or speedwork.

Strides

Strides are used by many runners as part of their warm-up, especially at the beginning of a track session. Striding is relaxed, fast running – a 'slow sprint', as one training manual puts it. The aim is to move across the ground as quickly as you can without straining yourself, concentrating on maintaining good form.

Strides can form a useful part of your speed training, as an alternative to repetitions and intervals. As with any running which is done at faster than your usual training pace, they educate your legs to cope with higher speeds. However, unlike with reps and intervals, you shouldn't time yourself when doing strides, or you could feel completely drained afterwards.

If you aren't on a track, pick a flat clear stretch of road or pavement where you won't lose your footing, before striding for a distance of between 100m and 400m. After each stride, walk or jog the same distance to recover.

Treadmills

While not a training principle, or even a training aid used by many elite runners, treadmills can be a useful addition to your fitness armour. A treadmill enables you to train during periods of bad weather when running outside is dangerous or simply impossible; a treadmill allows you to mimic conditions that you expect to find in a race, for example hills when you live in a completely flat area; a treadmill allows you to experiment with intervals and repetition running by enabling you to programme the exact efforts and recoveries that you want. On a treadmill, the weather is always the same, so you can more precisely see how – or if – you are improving.

Treadmill running is different from running outside: your body action changes slightly – you may find initially that you land more on your mid- or forefoot instead of your heel – but it is also less jarring than Tarmac, and there is no camber. However, treadmill running requires about seven per cent less energy than running outdoors – due to the lack of wind resistance – so you may think you are running faster than you really could do outside.

What about the boredom factor? Treadmills do remove one of the key benefits of running – being outside in the fresh air looking at the scenery – but the sheer monotony can also instill powers of concentration and discipline that you never knew you had. Or you can simply position yourself in front of the TV! The 1993 London Marathon winner, Eamonn Martin, prefers to do speedwork on a treadmill rather than a long run. One of his sample sessions is 10 x 1,000m at slightly faster than 10-kilometre pace, with two minutes' jogging in between each effort.

Sprint training

Unfortunately, much of the information in this book doesn't apply if you want to concentrate on the sprint events. A glance at a typical group of athletes at a track meeting will show you why: in terms of physique, the thin and wiry distance runners are worlds apart from the more obviously muscular sprinters.

However, you don't have to develop abs like Linford Christie's to be a successful sprinter; athletes of all shapes and sizes have become world-class 100m, 200m and 400m runners. Of course, it helps if you have some basic ability – a cart horse can never become a race horse, but it can become a swifter cart horse.

The sprints are physically and

technically challenging, demanding a combination of speed, strength, endurance (for the 400m) and skill. It's hard to acquire this on your own, and if you're serious about sprinting, you should join an athletics club, which will have specialist coaches to guide you through the strength work (including weight training, plyometrics and other exercises) and running drills you need.

It's worth thinking about which of the three sprints you want to specialise in, as the demands do vary:

100m

Even in a race that takes barely 10 seconds, there are four distinct phases:

1. At the gun you push hard out of the blocks, swinging your arms to gain momentum. Despite the power involved, you need to be relaxed in order to gain the control that ensures a good start.
2. For the first seven or eight steps, before you straighten up, your legs will be exerting more force on the ground that in the rest of the race. This is called the pick-up.
3. The force gives way to more agile motion as the feet begin to move more quickly. You should continue to accelerate until about halfway.
4. The challenge is to maintain maximum speed to the finish. Technique is crucial; you must maintain your form, however tired you feel.

200m

Many sprinters double up at the 100m and 200m, and the demands of the events are similar. However, the 200m does require more speed endurance, i.e. the capacity to maintain top speed for longer, and the acceleration phase is a little less frantic. Top runners generally complete the first 100 metres of the race about half a second slower than the second 100 metres.

The other main element of the 200m is bend running. Place your starting blocks at an angle which will allow you to run the first few strides in a straight line, and then lean into the bend, to counteract the centrifugal force which tends to make you skid outwards. It helps to be supple and relaxed, so that you can reach peak speed as you come into the straight.

400m

Although the 400m is still a sprint, the key to running it is to learn to distribute your energy economically. It's no use blasting round the first bend if you start to tie up before you reach the second; you should have enough energy left to pick up the pace in the third 100 metres. In the final straight, keep your stride long. Once again, you need to learn to relax so that you don't lose your form and waste energy. Your main enemy is the lactic acid which is produced by the demands of running so fast for so long. As well as muscular strength and speed, you need to work on lactic acid resistance by doing intensive interval sessions. If you take up this challenge, you'll soon learn why the 400m is known as 'the killer event'.

800/1,500 metre training

Training for these events calls for careful thinking and planning, mainly to develop the right balance between aerobic and anaerobic work, but also to include other elements such as speed, technique, tactics and, most importantly, mental 'toughness'.

Unless you're going to compete in indoor races (an option not available to most runners), you should divide your training into three phases:

1. The Endurance Phase: Approximately 20 weeks long, from October until the beginning of March.
2. The Pre-competition Phase: 12 weeks, from March until the end of May.
3. The Competition Period: Usually from early June until mid-September, a period of 14 weeks.

The endurance phase

This is the longest and is predominantly concerned with oxygen uptake. It takes longer to gain endurance than develop speed, but once gained it stays with you longer as you start to include the other elements.

It may seem a far cry from doing mainly steady-state running in the winter to speeding round in 800m or 1,500m races in the summer, but the colourful flowers of the track season owe their origin to the endurance seeds planted in winter. You will still continue to do some endurance work in the next two phases, but the bulk of it will have been done in this first phase.

The training threshold

As the vast amount of your running will be done aerobically, i.e. ensuring that oxygen uptake can meet the oxygen demands made during training, there will be very little build-up of lactic acid. Your training will be at a level high enough to produce a training effect, but not so high as to cause a build-up of lactic acid.

Your heart rate will give you a measure of the quality of your running and there is a 'training threshold' you must achieve for your training to be effective. To calculate your own training threshold:

1. Measure your heart beats per minute while lying in bed in the morning. Check for 10 seconds then multiply by six – this is your resting rate.
2. Measure your heart rate after a flat-out run over 200 or 300 metres. Again check for 10 seconds and multiply by six – this is your maximum rate. It may be difficult for you to do this after a flat-out run so get a friend to help you.
3. Deduct the resting pulse rate from the maximum and you have your pulse differential.
4. Calculate ⅔ of your pulse differential and add this figure to your resting rate – this is your training threshold rate.

For example, Fred has a resting rate of 60 beats per minute, and a maximum of 180 beats per minute. This gives a differential of 120 and ⅔ of this is 80. Add to his resting rate, and 140bpm is his training threshold – the minimum heart rate he should achieve during his training runs. Any less than this and there would be no training effect.

Of course, the heart rate changes to meet the speed of a run. As an example, Fred may do a short, fast run of 3–5 miles with a heart rate of 160–170bpm, but a longer run of 6–7 miles at 150–160bpm. You don't need to check every run, but it's a good idea to do so every so often to make sure you're achieving your training threshold.

As your body adapts to heavier training loads your heart rate may actually slow down – another reason to periodically recheck your training threshold.

Training rate and distances

Although a large part of your endurance work will be 'steady-state' and your heart rate will be fairly constant throughout, you can add variety in a number of ways. For example:

Do a run at a certain pace, have a short recovery jog then repeat the exercise several times. This prevents serious lactic build-up, but also prevents your heart rate from falling below your threshold during the recovery. This 'high-quality aerobic work' can be done with different distances – 3-minute runs with 30 seconds' recovery, or 5-minute efforts with one minute's recovery.

Distances for steady-state running can vary: 3–7 miles for an 800m runner and 3–12 miles for a 1,500m runner. Obviously longer runs are done at a slower pace than shorter distances – a 3-mile run in 18 minutes may be at 160–170bpm, while a 70-minute 10-mile run may be at 150–160bpm.

As with other training, start at a low level (both pace and distance) and build up during the winter. Be progressive rather than constant – don't stay too long at the same pace or distance.

A good coach will help you to achieve your very best.

ENDURANCE PHASE EXAMPLES

Beginners
October
Start by running 3 miles (M) every other day at a pace just above your training threshold. Increase this so that by the end of October you are running 5–6 miles every other day.

November	
Monday	5M steady
Tuesday	6M split: 4 steady, 1 easy, 1 steady
Wednesday	Rest
Thursday	6 repetitions round a flat 3-minute circuit, 3 minutes recovery
Friday	5M steady
Saturday	Rest
Sunday	7M steady

December	
Monday	5M steady
Tuesday	6M split: 1 fast, 3 steady, 1 easy, 1 fast
Wednesday	6x3-minute circuit, 2 minutes recovery
Thursday	Rest

Friday	5M steady
Saturday	4 reps round a flat 5-minute circuit, 3 minutes recovery
Sunday	7M easy/steady

January

Monday	Rest
Tuesday	6M steady
Wednesday	2 sets, 3x3-minute circuit, 30 seconds recovery, 3-minute recovery between sets
Thursday	6M easy
Friday	6M split: 2 fast, 2 steady, 1 easy, 1 fast
Saturday	Rest
Sunday	5x5-minute circuit, 3 minutes recovery. Alternate this session every other week to take part in a cross-country race

February

Monday	6M easy
Tuesday	6x3-minute circuit, 30 seconds recovery
Wednesday	6M steady
Thursday	6M split: 2 fast, 2 steady, 1 easy, 1 fast
Friday	Rest
Saturday	3x8-minute circuit, 3 minutes recovery. Alternate ever other week with a cross-country race
Sunday	7M steady, including 10x100m relaxed fast strides, with 100m-walk recovery

Advanced runners

October

Start by running 5 miles every day at a pace producing a heart rate just above your training threshold. Have a day's rest every four days. By the end of October you should have progressed to alternating 5-mile with 7-mile runs.

November

Monday	5M steady
Tuesday	7M split: 4M steady, 1 easy, 2 steady

Wednesday	6 reps round a flat 3-minute circuit, 2 minutes recovery
Thursday	7M steady
Friday	Rest
Saturday	45-minute fartlek
Sunday	8M steady, including 10x100m fast relaxed strides with 100m-walk recovery

December

Monday	5M steady
Tuesday	6x3-minute circuit, 1-minute recovery
Wednesday	8M steady
Thursday	8x600m track – a little slower than 1,500m race pace, 2 minutes recovery
Friday	Rest
Saturday	1 hour fartlek
Sunday	8M steady, including 10x100m fast strides

January

Monday	6M steady
Tuesday	8x3-minute circuit, 1-minute recovery
Wednesday	6M split: 1 fast, 3 steady, 1 easy, 1 fast
Thursday	8x600m (at about 1,500m race pace) with 90 seconds recovery
Friday	Rest
Saturday	1 hour fartlek, alternate every other week with cross-country race
Sunday	10M steady, including 10x100m strides

February

Monday	7M steady
Tuesday	2 sets 4x3-minute circuit, relaxed, 30 seconds recovery between circuits, 3 minutes recovery between sets
Wednesday	7M split: 1 fast, 4 steady, 1 easy, 1 fast
Thursday	2 sets 4x600m (1,500m race pace), 1-minute recovery between 600s, 3 minutes recovery between sets

Friday	Rest
Saturday	1 hour fartlek, alternate with cross-country race every other week
Sunday	12M steady, including 10x100m strides

During the endurance phase I would include a recuperation week in order to allow muscles to recover, and to ensure that your glycogen levels remain 'topped up'. In this week (last week in December is a good choice) just run 3 miles every other day if you're a beginner, while the more advanced can try 5 miles easy every other day.

The success of the endurance phase should be judged on the gradual build-up of regular training, with no special sessions, and no special weeks. You should be able to look back in March with pride on the volume of training done during the winter. But the ultimate test is whether or not you've improved your oxygen uptake.

The best way to ascertain this is to visit a physiology testing centre at the beginning of the phase, then re-visit in March. If there has been little or no improvement, then in following years the running in this period should be more intensive or over longer distances.

The pre-competition phase

This is the hardest training period. You must maintain endurance while at the same time bring on speed, speed endurance and race technique practice. The training becomes more intensive as you increase the speed of the repetitions and reduce recovery times. You will need to concentrate very hard during each session, but equally must learn to relax during the easier sessions and rest days.

During this period niggling injuries often crop up, so you would be wise to locate a sports-friendly doctor and an experienced physiotherapist. Often as you start doing more speedwork you get occasional stiffness in the legs – a good sports massage may help reduce this.

The balance between repetition speed and recovery time becomes crucial. If you go for quality in training, then the quantity will decrease and the recovery time becomes longer. During this time it's useful to have someone on hand to time your sessions, and, if possible, comment on your technique. Interval training will increase in importance – use the following as a rough guide to quantities, speeds and recovery times:

1. Quantity: You want to cover approximately twice the distance of your racing event, i.e. for 800m try 8x200m or 3x600m. For 1,500m try 8x400m or 4x800m.
2. Speed: Start at a pace slightly slower than your hoped-for race pace and gradually increase. If you're aiming for a 2:08 800m, start with 200m repetitions in 33 seconds, or 600m reps in 99 seconds.
   For the 1,500m runner aiming for 4 minutes, start with 66/67 seconds for 400m repetitions, and 2:13/2:14 for 800m reps. The target is to reduce these times down to 3–4 seconds faster than race pace.
3. Recovery times: Obviously this depends on the pace and the distance, but as a general rule you're ready for another effort once your pulse drops below 120bpm. Your heart rate at the end of each session should be above 280bpm.

SCHEDULE FOR BEGINNERS AND MORE ADVANCED RUNNERS

The make-up of the session is similar, but quality and quantity increases for more advanced runners.

First 3 weeks of period

Monday	6M steady
Tuesday	8x400m, 3 minute recovery
Wednesday	6M split: 2 fast, 2 steady, 1 easy, 1 fast
Thursday	4x600m, 4 minute recovery, then 10 minutes rest, then 10x100m fast strides with 100m walk recovery
Friday	Rest
Saturday	6 repetitions round a 3-minute undulating grass circuit, 3 minute recovery
Sunday	7M steady

Second 3 weeks of period

Monday	6M steady
Tuesday	8x400m (2–3 seconds faster than previous period), 3 minutes recovery
Wednesday	6M split: 2 fast, 3 steady, 1 fast
Thursday	6x600m (2–3 seconds faster than previous period), 4 minutes recovery, 10 minutes rest, 10x100m fast strides with 100m walk recovery
Friday	Rest
Saturday	6x3-minute circuit (4–5 seconds faster than previous period), 3 minutes recovery
Sunday	7M steady

Seventh week of period
This is a regeneration week: just do a short easy run each day followed by 5/6 relaxed strides over 100m.

Weeks 8/9/10 for 800m specialist

Monday	6M steady
Tuesday	6x300m (2–3 seconds faster than projected race pace for this distance, 2 minutes recovery. Then 6x60m fast strides – walk back between each.
Wednesday	5M split: 3 fast, 1 easy, 1 fast
Thursday	3x600m (2–3 seconds faster than projected race pace for this distance), 5–6 minutes recovery
Friday	Rest
Saturday	4x3-minute circuit fast, 5–6 minutes recovery, then 10 minutes rest, then 8x100m fast strides
Sunday	6M steady

Weeks 11/12 for 800m specialist

Monday	6M steady
Tuesday	5x300m (a little faster than previously), 5–6 minutes recovery, 10 minutes rest, then 6x60m sprint, walk back between each
Wednesday	4M fairly fast relaxed run
Thursday	1x1,000m (just slower than race pace), 6 minutes recovery. 2x600m (at race pace), 5–6 minutes recovery, 4x200m (2 seconds faster than race pace), 2–3 minutes recovery
Friday	Rest
Saturday	Race practice – 3x800m split: 400m in 2–3 seconds faster than race pace, 200m jog, 200m fast, 7–8 minutes recovery, 20 minutes rest, 8x100m fast strides
Sunday	6M split: 2 fast, 2 steady, 1 easy, 1 fast

Weeks 8/9/10 for 1,500m specialist

Monday	6M steady
Tuesday	6x500m (a little faster than race pace), 4–5 minutes recovery, 20 minutes rest, 6x150m acceleration run (start off easily, gradually build up speed and sprint the last 20–30m – walk back in between)
Wednesday	6M split: 1 fast, 4 steady, 1 fast
Thursday	4x800m at race pace, 4–5 minutes recovery, 10 minutes rest, 10x100m fast, relaxed strides, walk back in between
Friday	Rest
Saturday	6x3-minutes circuit fairly fast but relaxed, 90 seconds recovery
Sunday	8M steady run

Weeks 11/12 for 1,500m runner

Monday	6M steady
Tuesday	6x400m (3–4 seconds faster than race pace), 4–5 minutes recovery, 20 minutes rest, 10x100m fast strides
Wednesday	5M fairly fast relaxed run
Thursday	3x1,000m (just a little slower than race pace), 7–8 minutes recovery, 20 minutes rest, 6x150m acceleration runs
Friday	Rest
Saturday	Race practice – 3x1,200m split: 1st 800m 2 seconds faster than race pace, 200m jog, 200m fast, 7–8 minutes recovery
Sunday	8M relaxed run

The competition period

Obviously the key aim in this period is to perform well in races. The training is still of high quality but tapers off for a few days before each race, and should not be so intensive that you go into a race feeling tired. Concentrate on being relaxed – a good way to do this is to run repetitions at the same pace as before but in a more relaxed way.

The aim is to be able to say to yourself at the end of the session that you could have run much faster if needed. That need will come in races. 'Relaxed' means trying to run without any tension in arms, neck or shoulders, not running slowly or sloppily.

The frequency of racing is an individual thing – some runners like to race every week, others need longer to recover. One of the snags in racing frequently is that, in tapering down before the day, and going easy in training afterwards, you actually lose quite a lot of training. On the other hand, racing will bring the best out of you and will teach you tactics. Your training will attempt to make you an all-round racer, i.e. a runner who can lead the race at a fast pace and attempt to shake off other runners; or a runner who is happier sitting in behind the leaders, waiting to produce a fast finish.

The ability to finish fast depends upon having a high enough oxygen uptake to arrive at the closing stages of a race with something in reserve. You then need the technique to sprint, and that technique is going to depend a lot on flexibility, especially in the hips and ankles, and strength.

I suggest doing high knee lifts by running slowly on the spot – this strengthens both hamstrings and quadriceps. Ensure that you lift your legs straight – don't let them point outwards.

You can strengthen calves and ankles by doing heel-raising exercises on the track curb. Strong legs will help you lift up high at the end of a race, and prevent your knees pointing out. To avoid injury and unnecessary energy expenditure, you need to plant your feet in a straight line – try to practise this during your strides and acceleration runs.

A 10-day cycle between races is a good compromise as follows:

10-DAY CYCLE BETWEEN 800M RACES

1. 5M steady
2. 3x600m split: 400m fast, 100m jog, 100m fast, 5–6 minutes recovery, 20 minutes rest, 10x100m strides
3. 4x300m very fast, 7–8 minutes recovery, 3M easy run
4. 30 minutes fartlek
5. 3x400m quite fast, 6–7 minutes recovery, 20 minutes rest, 6x150m acceleration runs
6. 5M run split: 1 fast, 3 steady, ½ easy, ½ fast
7. 6x200m at race pace – 200m jog recovery

8. Rest
9. Race
10. 6M easy run, 10 minutes rest, 10x100m relaxed strides

10-DAY CYCLE BETWEEN 1500M RACES

1. 6M steady
2. 3x1,200m split: 800m fast, 200m easy, 200m fast, 7–8 minutes recovery, 20 minutes rest, 10x100m fast strides
3. 7M steady run
4. 3x800m (race pace), 8–10 minutes recovery, 20 minutes rest, 4x150m acceleration runs
5. 5M easy run
6. 6x400m fast (2–3 seconds faster than race pace), 4–5 minutes recovery
7. 8x200m relaxed, 200m jog recovery
8. Rest
9. Race
10. 8M easy run, 10 minutes rest, 10x100m relaxed strides

As regards races, try to alternate racing at your specialist distance with over- and under-distance races. For example, an 800m runner should race over 400m and 1,500m, while a 1,500m runner could alternate 800m and 3,000m races.

5,000/10,000 metre training

By definition, training for the two longest distance track events has traditionally been the preserve of distance running. Most approaches to the 5,000m and 10,000m tend to treat them as a pair, much as the 800m and 1,500m are thought of together. The training has traditionally followed that approach. History clearly throws forth many successful examples to back up the logic of this argument: the great Finnish distance runner, Lasse Viren, his Olympic successor, Miruts Yifter, or even closer to home, Brendan Foster. They all ran with great success over both distances. Over the last 10–15 years those barriers have been broken down as people have started to come to the 5,000m from a 1,500m background. Dave Moorcroft was the first, followed by Said Aouita and, most recently, Venuste Niyongabo, who had only run three 5,000m races before he took the Olympic title in Atlanta. The ability of runners to cross the boundaries has been proven and training methods have adapted to this change as runners have shown that they can mature through the training. While many traditional approaches have tended to stress the endurance of the 10,000m, I think the speed of the 5,000m is more critical. That is not to suggest that the endurance is not important, but the more difficult race of the two is the shorter, faster event which has to be accounted for in your training.

Endurance is important, but speed is the key to both 5,000m and 10,000m racing.

Basic principles

The training principles outlined in the 800/1,500m chapter hold true for much of your training here. The year again breaks down into three phases: the endurance conditioning phase, the pre-competition phase and competition phase.

Endurance phase

Many of the training sessions are similar to those of the middle distances with one major exception: you will need to make the overall programme more endurance-based. You will need to increase the mileage and start to perform on the roads. In many ways the track athlete has to be the ultimate performer, transferring the endurance lessons from road and cross-country to the track. So within this period the mileage should be higher, concentrating predominantly on steady consistent training as your base. Within that base is the need to demonstrate versatility with longer performances up to 10 miles and half-marathon. Cross-country is not a requirement for success but it is a great background. Someone like David Moorcroft had his great year in 1982 and I don't think it was any coincidence that it was the same year he also finished second in the National Cross-country. In my own experience when I had good track years they came off strong winter performances: when I ran 13:10 for 5,000m, for example, I had also finished second in the National Cross-country Championships earlier in the year.

That endurance base is important. For beginners introducing themselves to the distances, you should think about a weekly mileage up to 50 miles per week, including track-based sessions; for the advanced runners a weekly total around 80 miles per week, training twice a day, four or five days a week. You should also add to that two or three sessions a week in the gym to improve your overall body conditioning, which at a more modest level is something the beginner would also benefit from. A good athlete is a well conditioned athlete.

Also try to balance the surfaces and balance quantity against quality through the winter months. As a general guide, start the circuits in October; November should still be an easy month, and increase intensity for January and February.

ENDURANCE PHASE EXAMPLE SESSIONS

Beginners
October
Build up to 5 miles 6 times per week

November onwards

Sunday	75-minute run
Monday	30 minutes a.m.
Tuesday	30 minutes a.m.
	Track p.m.
Wednesday	45-minute run
Thursday	Road run 5–10 miles, 75 per cent effort
Friday	30 minutes
Saturday	Grass-training session 30 minutes

Sample track session
4x1 minute (3 minutes recovery)
16 laps continuous run (200m fast, 200m slow)

Sample grass session
12 x long hill up to 200m, jog-back recovery
5x3 minutes hard (2 minutes recovery)

Advanced
October
Build up to 7 miles 6 times per week

November–February

Sunday	90-minute up to 2-hour run
Monday	30 minutes a.m.
	30 minutes p.m.
Tuesday	30 minutes a.m.
	Track session p.m.
Wednesday	60 minutes
Thursday	60 minutes 5–10-mile road run,
	80 per cent effort
Friday	30 minutes
Saturday	Grass session – 30 minutes

Sample track sessions
6x1 mile (2-minute recovery)
24 laps continuous run (200m fast, 200 slow)

Sample grass sessions
6x300m uphill (jog back recovery)
6x4 minutes (3-minute recovery)

Pre-competition phase

This is the period of transition, a transition from strong well-conditioned athlete to performance track athlete. It's a change that has to be made gradually. The biggest potential problem is injury, brought about by trying to do too much too quickly. You should be looking for a steady transition by gradually increasing the number and intensity of your faster repetitions.

You should aim for a period of training at or below your race pace. The 5,000m is 12.5 laps of the track; you have to think carefully about the pace and the different speeds that you will be attempting. If you want to be comfortable doing a 15-minute 5,000m then you need to be able to do 72-second laps; you will never break 20 minutes if a 95-second lap is tough. If you can't relax at sustained pace then you have trouble.

One of the problems that many athletes find difficult to cope with is the pace of 5,000m; that's particularly the case if their training has never sustained periods at race pace. You need to be capable of getting to 3,000m comfortably.

If you can't then you have a problem. If you want to do 34 minutes for 10,000m then you need to be able to run 17 minutes for 5,000m with ease.

EXAMPLE SESSIONS

Beginners
November onwards

Sunday	75-minute run

March–May

Sunday	1-hour run
Monday	30 minutes a.m.
Tuesday	Track session
Wednesday	30 minutes
Thursday	Lighter track session plus gentle run
Friday	30 minutes
Saturday	Grass session 30 minutes

Sample track sessions
12x400m (1-minute recovery) or 1,000m steady, 2-minute recovery, 400m fast x 2

Sample of lighter track sessions
8x300m (2-minute recovery) or 3x600m (5-minute recovery)

Sample grass sessions
6x2-minute run (2-minute recovery)

Advanced
March–May

Sunday	1 hour 30-minute run
Monday	30 minutes a.m.
	30 minutes p.m.
Tuesday	30 minutes a.m.
	Track session p.m.
Wednesday	60 minutes
Thursday	30 minutes
	Lighter track session pm.
Friday	30 minutes
Saturday	Grass sessions 30 minutes

Sample track sessions
12x400m (1-minute recovery) or 1,000m steady, 1-minute recovery, 400m fast (5-minute recovery) x 3 or 1,200m steady, 1-minute recovery, 400m fast (5-minute recovery) x 3

Sample grass sessions
6x1 minute (1-minute recovery)
8x2 minutes (1-minute recovery)

Examples of lighter track sessions
8x300m (1-minute jog recovery)
6x400m (3-minute recovery)

Competition phase

Don't lose touch with the distance below your goal. You have to be able to perform at distances shorter than your race distance. Good 10,000m runners need to be good 5,000m runners and good 5,000m runners should be good milers. There is no other way to improve in these

What can you learn from the domination of the Africans?

In recent years the road and track scene has been dominated by African runners, predominantly from the East and the North. While there are certain factors which afford them physiological advantages, such as an early life often spent running at altitude, there are two other psychological factors which give an edge to their performances:

1. African runners have no constraints in their minds. The Western approach to life is more disciplined. It is part of our social conditioning to see targets ahead of us, which can be limits as much as goals, and we set out a plan to overcome them in a gradual, measured way. The African runner performs with more joy and spontaneity and is more likely to go with a pace or a race even if it is outside their perceived abilities. Sometimes it goes wonderfully well, other times it goes horribly wrong. With our societal conditioning it is hard to break away from our 'natural' more cautious approach, but try to.

2. African runners have no fear of failure. To the winner go the accolades, that's it. To their mind there are no losers, they just didn't win. There is no psychological stigma to a bad run or a race that went appallingly wrong. It is part of a high-risk strategy, which sometimes reaps rewards and sometimes doesn't. The important thing is that they start the next race with the same mental attitude as the previous one. The performances are not as consistent, but the highs are much higher.

areas than to race over the distance. During a season committed to 5,000m the ideal balance should be 3–5 5,000m races, 3–4 3,000m races and 3–4 1,500m races. With 10,000m, for which you need more recovery time, you should aim to run twice over the race distance, 2–3 times over 5,000m and 2–3 3,000m runs.

Dave Moorcroft, for example, broke the 5,000m world record after running his best 1,500m in Oslo earlier in the year. In the season in which I won the European 5,000m, I ran my best 3,000m and 1,500m earlier that year.

Versatility and the ability to cope with changes of pace and race tactics are something that has to be practised and duplicated in training. There are many athletes who can run fast times in a steady paced race but just can't cope with a change of pace. When you come to step out on the track for the first time, remind yourself how many laps you have to run: four laps is a mile, eight is two, twelve is three. Try to translate that into a time per lap, 70 seconds is 14:20; 80 seconds is

16:40; 90 seconds is 18:38 for 5,000m. Over the longer distance, 75 seconds is 31:15 and 90 seconds is 37:15. Keep your eye on the lap counter and be aware of what pace you are running at and how far you are going.

Beginners

June–August
Aim to compete between 6–10 times

Sunday	1-hour run
Monday	30 minutes
Tuesday	30 minutes
	Track p.m.
Wednesday	45 minutes
Thursday	30 minutes
Friday	Rest
Saturday	Grass session or race

Sample track sessions
10x400m (2-minute recovery)
4x600m (1-minute recovery)

Grass sessions as in previous phase

Advanced

June–August

Sunday	1-hour run
Monday	30 minutes a.m.
	30 minutes p.m.
Tuesday	30 minutes a.m.
	Track session p.m.
Wednesday	45 minutes
Thursday	30 minutes a.m.
	30 minutes p.m.
Friday	30 minutes
Saturday	Grass session or race

Sample track sessions
12x400m (1-minute recovery)
4x600m (3-minute recovery)

Sample grass sessions
8x2 minutes (1-minute recovery)
10xuphill 150m, jog-back recovery

K ey principles

1. Always take two or three days easy before competition.
2. Always take two or three days easy after competition.
3. Don't build up too quickly.
4. Be prepared to stop and see a physiotherapist whenever there is a hint of an injury.
5. Watch your diet.
6. Follow a gentle stretching programme.
7. All-round body conditioning will improve performance.

Road running

Running is little more than going the distance as quickly as possible. In road running, the distance is never very short, and the pure speed of a sprinter won't get you all the way. Speed is an invaluable asset to a road runner and greatly widens tactical capabilities, but endurance, or stamina, is the basis of the discipline.

Just to cover the distance while maintaining a running action is the minimum ambition of many a runner entering events for the first time. This is particularly true of the marathon, but this event places its own special demands on the body which are discussed in Chapter 9. In road running, distances may range from five kilometres (just over three miles) to twenty miles. Different preparation may be required for each end of the range, but it is mainly a question of emphasis within similarly structured training programmes.

Speed and endurance are the raw materials of running. Most training is aimed at developing one or the other, or even both at the same time. Other things are required to help blend these ingredients into the fullest capability.

Concentration is needed to keep up

Pace judgement is important in every kind of training run.

maximum effort. People often ask, 'But what do you think about all the time?' It could be almost anything if you are jogging at less than serious effort. If you are trying to get the most out of yourself you have to concentrate – and think about that task almost exclusively. If your mind wanders during a series of 400m intervals (see below), for example, you will soon notice that the lap times have slipped as a result.

Any children's race, no matter what the distance, usually begins and ends with a big sprint. But it's what happens in between that counts. The start and finish are a small part of road races, and easiest to concentrate on – especially when there's a crowd to impress. Concentrating isn't enough to get your best effort out, though. You have to have a finely tuned sense of pace judgment to know how fast you should be going, so that you don't either tire too soon or have too much in reserve at the finish.

Pace judgement is often instinctive, but you can attune your instinct by practice. Repeating hard runs and trying to maintain consistent times for them is a standard form of training (interval or repetition training), and it cultivates your sense of what average pace you can sustain over different distances.

Although pace judgement is a virtue, and an even pace will generally be the best way to record your fastest possible time for any particular distance, there will be times when it needs to be overridden. Advantage may be gained by a sudden injection of speed – to get quickly clear of someone before they can respond, for instance. Race tactics can easily run wild, though. They are best employed sparingly, when you sense that they will tell more on the opponent than on yourself.

Elements of training

Training should improve form by working on speed, stamina and strength, with emphasis depending on what you aim to achieve. Concentration and pace judgement will be required to complete the training, but tactical sense will be gained from racing.

If going the distance is the limit of your ambition, endurance is the only element of training that need be of concern. Once the distance or further has been run in training (a long run), there is no reason why it cannot be repeated in a race.

A race is an odd situation in which to find yourself. Your ambitions, fixed beforehand, suddenly start changing by the minute. There are other people all around to stimulate your competitive instincts. Suddenly, it's no longer enough just to get to the finish line; you want to beat a friend, or any anonymous runner who passed you earlier in the race.

Besides, once you have completed a fixed race distance, like 10 kilometres or the half-marathon, you will want to improve on it next time. Speed becomes a key concern.

To increase your speed over the full race distance you will need to get used to running faster over shorter distances. You might do this in two different ways: by running continuously for, say, half the race distance (a pace run); or by running repeatedly over much shorter distances, say 5–10 per cent of the race distance (intervals of repetition training). The pace run can be done easily enough by entering some shorter races. The interval session requires you to bring a self-imposed discipline to your training.

Sprinters do intervals too, but they will go at top speed for very short distances and have a long recovery. Road runners do intervals not to gain pure speed, but speed endurance. How much speed, and how much endurance, depends on the length of the target race, and this in turn will affect the number of repetitions, and the recovery (length and type of rest) between them. The length of the repetitions will probably vary less: most road runners will range between 400m and 1 mile. Although shorter repetitions are also useful, they contribute less directly to speed endurance.

We have identified several distinct types of training session: a long run, a pace run, and interval training. There are other possibilities:

Hill training helps to build strength and muscular co-ordination, but may be considered a particular form of interval training.

Fartlek is a particular type of interval training, usually over varied terrain, where the distances run at speed may range widely.

A pyramid session combines intervals and recoveries of varying length, increasing and then decreasing their distance (or time) and adjusting the speed accordingly. This is a good exercise for pace judgement.

Intervals and the pace run may be done one after the other in a combination session. This is particularly useful in training for longer races, where race pace has to be maintained when the runner is already fatigued. At least every other day runners train 'easily' (recovery running), at a pace which does not stress their bodies enough to impede recovery from the 'hard' sessions.

Training schedules for improving performance should combine these essential elements: long run; pace run; intervals. Between these 'key' sessions, training will consist of rest or recovery running. Beyond equal spacing of effort throughout the week there are no fixed rules to follow. Most people do long runs on Sundays, when not racing, because they have more time available and it is possible to run with others. Most clubs or training groups meet on Tuesdays or Thursdays for interval sessions; not too close to weekend races or long runs, but allowing a gap to fit one other hard training session into the week. These arrangements may suit a majority, but they may not suit you. You must carefully weigh the demands of your working and social life to see how and when you can fit in the effort of training.

Training schedules

A training schedule is a planned series of training sessions which are aimed at maintaining or improving performance, whether in competition or not. Two questions immediately arise: what is the event to be performed, and what level of performance is to be improved upon?

Road races start from 5 kilometres, and may stretch to 20 miles. Anything less than 5 kilometres is most likely to be called a 'fun run', and anything more is marathon or ultra territory. But one runner's fun run is another's race. Fun runs are an extremely useful innovation which allow beginner runners to gain the experience and confidence necessary to enter more traditional races.

Within these limits road races can be any distance. The majority, though, are carefully measured standard distances: 5, 10, 15, 20, 25 and 30 kilometres; 5, 6, 10, 15 and 20 miles; and the half-marathon. By far the most popular distances are 10 kilometres, 10 miles and half-marathon. For this reason they are used here as conveniently spaced pegs upon which to hang generalised schedules. Suggestions will be made on how to adapt these to longer or shorter races.

We have already listed the main elements of a training schedule, and how they are typically fitted together. Schedules will vary in detailed content according to the specific distance and also the level of performance. The biggest differences between performers at the same distance, though, will be in the intensity at which the training is done.

Ready to race?

After a few weeks 'getting started' you will be able to follow a schedule something like this:

Sunday	60 minutes of running and walking.
Tuesday	5-minute warm-up; 3 minutes hard running followed by 2 minutes recovery, repeated 4 times (4 x 3', 2' recovery); 5-minute warm-down.
Thursday	5-minute warm-up; 15-minute pace run; 5-minute warm-down.
Saturday	25-minute run (* see 'General', p. 53 following schedules below).

When you can do this you should try to run some 5-kilometre races. If you lack confidence why not try a 2- or 3-mile fun run at full effort to get yourself used to racing.

Road race distances may vary sixfold; the training is usually more constant. For longer race distances the long run may be barely the same length but, at the other end of the scale, a long run might be three times as long as a short race. Sprinters occasionally do 2-mile runs; middle-distance track runners may do 8 or 10 miles. Training for 5-kilometre races, a long run of 10 miles is still worthwhile; for 10-kilometre races it is advisable; for 10-mile races it is a minimum; and for a half-marathon it is probably insufficient.

Training for a 10-kilometre race

This is now the main racing distance in Britain. Once runners only wanted to do a race with the word 'marathon' in its title. Now wiser, we realise that 10-kilometre races are useful in preparation for longer races, and cause far less disruption to our training and our lives in general.

Sunday	10-mile run.
Tuesday	7-minute warm-up; 5 x 3', 2' recovery; 7-minute warm-down.
Thursday	7-minute warm-up; 25-minute pace run; 7-minute warm-down.
Saturday	40-minute run.

The main task is to work up to a long run of 10 miles. If you are new to running you may find concentration difficult for such a long period. Keep it enjoyable. Don't try to get it over as quickly as you can, and 'burn out' early in the run; walk if necessary. Keep it interesting; ten miles can take you to some unfamiliar places and back. Don't just repeat short laps, or even do the same route every week; vary your route, and plan it out on a map. Keep it purposeful. You may want to get dropped, or take a train to a point 10 miles away and then run home to a big late breakfast (don't eat too much before you train, see Chapter 15).

The interval session should not be the same every week. Five efforts of three minutes is given as an indication of an appropriate workload. Try four efforts of four minutes, three of five, or seven of two minutes. Your speed will adjust to the interval distance, further adjusted instinctively according to the number of repetitions you anticipate doing. Speed will, though, always be greater than your race pace or the speed of your pace run. Note that the length is not measured by distance. Although top runners will do interval training on the track, it can be just as effective on grass. The main difference is that on a track you know exactly how far you have run, on grass you will only have a general idea. After several sessions, if you start all your efforts in the same position and follow the same route, you will have a much closer idea. It may be too close for comfort. Don't compete against the previous week's times – it is a waste of effort.

The pace run should also be varied. Again, it will be faster than race pace but the length is suggested as an indication. Vary it between 20 and 30 minutes from week to week, and take different routes.

Training for a 10-mile race

Before marathons became popular, 10 miles used to be the main road race distance. Even now, if a '10' is advertised, it means miles not kilometres.

Sunday	12–13-mile run.
Tuesday	10-minute warm-up; 5 x 4', 2' recovery; 10-minute warm-down.
Thursday	10-minute warm-up; 30–35-minute pace run; 10-minute warm-down.
Saturday	40-minute run.*

You could do a 10-mile race off the 10-kilometre schedule without suffering distress. Why, then, go to the bother of doing more than that? To race regularly over 10 miles, the 10-kilometre schedule would leave you inadequately prepared. You would have to curtail training between races to recover more fully after them – and rest up more before them. With the above schedule you will be better able to take them in your stride, and you will also be able to improve your performance.

The length of the long run should be kept above the race distance by a margin that will inspire confidence. Keep week-to-week variation in both the interval and pace sessions: any combination of intervals that total 18–20 minutes of hard running, and pace runs of between 20–40 minutes will meet your general requirements. You could try building the intervals into a pyramid pattern, running, for example, 3', 4', 5', 4', 3'. Take recovery times half as long as the effort just completed.

Training for a half-marathon

Sunday	15-mile run.
Tuesday	15-minute warm-up; 6 x 4', 2' recovery; 15-minute warm-down.
Thursday	15-minute warm-up; 40-minute pace run; 15-minute warm-down.
Saturday	45-minute run.*

Again, you could run an occasional half-marathon off the 10-mile schedule. The training above will prepare you sufficiently to do them regularly and to compete occasionally at longer distances, up to 20 miles. With relatively minor adjustments this schedule would be appropriate for a full marathon, but there are other factors involved in racing distances over 20 miles which deserve special consideration (see Chapter 9).

General

The above schedules are illustrative. They may suit some people in their entirety, but most people will want to adapt them to their own needs.

As a general guide, the above schedules will mean running about 19–27 miles a week for a 10-kilometre competition,

24–34 miles for a 10-mile competition, and 31–42 miles for the half-marathon. Most of the variation in the mileage will be if you include the Saturday run or not.

(*) The Saturday run is not an essential 'element' to training, and may be dispensed with if you wish. By contrast, you may wish to run on days between those 'key' sessions suggested above. If you do so, keep the running at an easy pace or you will feel tired when it comes to running the harder sessions. If you do want to run on these rest (or 'recovery') days, start off with 15 minutes of very easy running on one of them. Add more days before you increase the duration. Keep one day (probably Monday or Friday) free of training.

Races

Training may become boring if you are fixed on too distant a goal. It may help to focus your training more effectively if you enter races at regular intervals. These can act as short-term incentives to keep you on track with your training and allow you to see improvements or identify remaining weaknesses in your competitive armoury.

If you do have an overall target that you wish to achieve, don't let the stepping-stone races towards that target become too important. Don't pack in races for which you continually have to interrupt your normal training. Races will unfailingly be 'hard' sessions, even when you intend only to run easily in them. They will be more significant than any training session, not least because you are performing publicly. You will make more effort to put on a good show without even realising it. Allow yourself adequate time to recover before starting to train hard again. Plan races into your training.

A race every second week is probably enough for most people and some will prefer to race more sparingly. One reason for racing more frequently would be if you find it difficult to fit hard training into your working week. If you use races to substitute for hard training like this, and train lightly between them, make sure the races are appropriate. Don't enter them indiscriminately. Races are organised as single events, whereas you will need to string them together in a logical sequence which serves your own training purposes.

Marathon training

Whatever the historical quirk that led to the distance being set at 26 miles and 285 yards, two things are accepted about the marathon – first, it's rightly referred to as the 'personal Everest' because of the physical and mental demands it places on elite runner and jogger alike; second, it's a very long way.

But it is an achievable goal, as many thousands of all shapes and sizes prove every year. But whether you finish one and feel able to start planning for another, or whether your experience is painful beyond belief and puts you off for all time will depend very much on the training you've put in.

The marathon distance must be treated with respect. Of course there are always stories of people who get round in three hours with no training, but for most of us this is simply not possible. With time and effort put into the proper training, the marathon experience can be one of the most exhilarating that running has to offer.

The type of training you do depends very much on the level of runner you are, and what you're expecting from your marathon in terms of time. Whatever

Nothing will prepare you fully for the marathon experience.

your goal, you really need to have been running regularly before even thinking about attempting a marathon, and preferably in regular training for at least a year.

Fifteen years ago there were well over 130 marathons to choose from in the UK; now the number is around 30. A big city marathon, like London with 27,000 runners, is very different from a smaller race with 1,000 competitors. There are advantages to both: a big race like London or New York delivers atmosphere, crowds and the feeling of having completed one of the world's great courses; a smaller race enables you to run your race in a way that's probably more similar to how you've trained – you won't need to dodge and weave round your fellow competitors, and you won't have to wait for long to get across the start line.

Whichever race you choose, you need to do so some months in advance and then start to plan your training. A race like the London Marathon has an entry limit and more apply to run than are accepted. You will have to apply some months in advance, and usually hear if you've been successful in mid-December, about four months before the race. For a smaller race, entry is usually no problem, and *Runner's World* will provide details of upcoming races well in advance. You should try to find out something about the course from the race organiser – you don't want to find at the last minute that it's all uphill and off-road unless that's what you wanted.

Depending on your current level of fitness, 12–16 weeks is long enough to train specifically for a marathon. If you practise other sports, they may help your level of overall fitness, but fitness for running can really only be gained by running. Fitness for a marathon, indeed keeping yourself healthy for the months of hard training ahead, is also a specific requirement, because the effort will place extra demands upon your system.

Running a healthy marathon

There are two basic rules to keeping healthy during your marathon build-up. First, eat more. Second, sleep more. For every mile of additional training, you should eat 100 extra calories. For example, if you're increasing your weekly mileage from 30 to 50, you need at least 2,000 more calories each week, or 300 per day. Primarily this will keep your blood sugar levels from dropping, leading to feelings of listlessness and irritability. If you can, though, don't tuck into the extra calories last thing at night, which will mean they will be stored as fat. Try rather to eat within two hours of finishing your training, when it's easier for your body to store fuel as carbohydrate. *(See also Chapter 15.)*

In full marathon training, try to sleep an extra hour per night. You're putting an unnatural demand on your body, and your normal sleep pattern just won't be able to cope. Additionally, take one full rest day each week, and try to cut back as much as possible on family and work commitments. This is easier said than done, but, although marathon training is demanding, it is also finite – there is a life to go back to afterwards.

If you're training for a spring marathon, the bulk of your training will be done during the winter, when it's more likely that you'll catch some sort of cold or virus. Training hard makes you more vulnerable, but you can take some precautions. Taking 500mg of Vitamin C can cut in half your chances of a respiratory infection. Try to avoid people with colds, wash your hands before eating and dry them with hot air rather than towels if possible to reduce the chances of picking up an infection.

Lastly, increase your fluid intake on a regular basis, not just during and after training. Drink a cupful of water every time you pass the water fountain at work, or at least once per hour.

Training

Now that your health is OK for the duration of the training period, it's down to the training itself. The core session for every marathon runner is the long run. Whether you're just planning to get round the course, or you're hoping for a good time, the long run is a vital ingredient. For beginners, the long run represents the best way for the body to get acquainted with being on the move for, ultimately, several hours. For faster runners, an increasingly important element is quality work, learning how to develop speed endurance, but the long run is still best for developing endurance.

You should be following a training schedule, either being helped by more experienced runners or best of all a coach at your running club, or using schedules which appear in *Runner's World* every year. Try to stick to the schedule, but be realistic: if you're ill, or feel you're overdoing it, ease back. Far better to have an easy week than to lose two weeks of training through illness or injury.

As a general rule, don't increase your mileage by more than 10 per cent from one week to the next. Sudden increases in mileage can be a shock to your system and place unwanted stresses on joints and muscles. If you're a relative newcomer to running, be prepared for marathon training to take up a large part of your life. If you can, set aside regular times to train – for example, running to and from work is a good way of building up the miles. If you get an injury, don't

try to run through it. Assess the situation realistically, and get appropriate medical advice. The increase in mileage can take its toll, as you force your body to make the same repetitive movement over hundreds of miles. Get a regular massage if you can; reduce inflammation, if any, after running by putting ice on the affected area; make sure your shoes are not worn out and are giving you enough support and cushioning. Try to run off-road as much as possible, as grass is a much more forgiving surface than Tarmac, although be careful not to twist an ankle.

Sample schedules

In *Runner's World*, marathon schedules are divided up into three bands to cater for the novice, more experienced, and very experienced runner. The schedule below runs over 14 weeks and is calculated on time, not miles per week. While it is impossible to design a schedule that suits everyone individually down to the smallest detail, it is possible to offer flexible guidelines which produce results.

The key is flexibility: as a general rule each schedule follows overall principles, while allowing for possible illness or tiredness which may affect training. As a basic guide to training pace, use the following guide: *Easy* – a recovery run or slow jog; *Slow* – slower than your expected marathon pace; *Steady* – roughly your marathon pace; *Brisk* – your half-marathon pace; *Fast* – your 10K pace or faster.

Novice schedule

This is designed for someone who is not currently running a great deal, who does not have a great deal of time to devote to training and whose ambition is simply to complete the course.

The key principle is to run four days a

week, and to build up the long run each weekend. There is a certain amount of 'quality' work built in which will help you improve running speed. You can take rest days between each running day, but you will have to run two days consecutively once a week.

Week 1
Day 1   20 minutes easy
Day 2   20 minutes easy
Day 3   20 minutes easy
Day 4   1 hour walk/jog e.g. 10 minutes jog, 5 minutes walk

Week 2
Day 1   20 minutes easy
Day 2   25 minutes easy
Day 3   20-25 minutes easy
Day 4   1 hour walk/jog, trying to jog more

Week 3
Day 1   25 minutes easy
Day 2   25 minutes easy
Day 3   25 minutes easy
Day 4   80–90 minutes jog/walk

Week 4
Day 1   25 minutes easy
Day 2   20 minutes, including 6 faster bursts of 50 metres
Day 3   25 minutes easy
Day 4   Race of 10K–10M, with 10 minutes jog before

Week 5
Day 1   25 minutes easy
Day 2   25 minutes, including 5 minutes at faster pace
Day 3   25 minutes easy
Day 4   90–100 minutes jog/walk

Week 6
Day 1   25 minutes easy
Day 2   30 minutes, including 6x1-minute surges
Day 3   25 minutes steady
Day 4   100 minutes jog/walk

Week 7
Day 1   25 minutes easy
Day 2   5 minutes easy including some short bursts
Day 3   35 minutes, including 2x5 minutes faster pace
Day 4   1 hour running – try not to walk

Week 8
Day 1   25 minutes steady
Day 2   25 minutes, including 5x1-minute fast with jog recovery
Day 3   25 minutes easy
Day 4   2 hours, walk last 5 minutes of first hour and first 5 minutes of second hour

Week 9
Day 1   25 minutes easy
Day 2   30 minutes, including 6x1-minute fast with jog recovery
Day 3   25 minutes steady
Day 4   80–90 minutes jog, or half-marathon

Week 10
Day 1   25 minutes easy
Day 2   20 minutes, including 2x1-minute fast, 2 minutes slow, then 5 fast
Day 3   25 minutes steady, including 5x1-minute fast
Day 4   150 minutes jog/walk – take it very easy

Week 11
Day 1   20 minutes easy
Day 2   20 minutes, including 6x1-minute fast, 1 minute slow
Day 3   20 minutes, including 3 minutes faster
Day 4   2 hours, walking last 5 minutes of first hour and first 5 minutes of second

Week 12
Day 1   20 minutes easy
Day 2   25–30 minutes, including 8x1-minute fast, 1 minute slow
Day 3   25 minutes easy
Day 4   Half-marathon, with 1M jog before and after – total 15M

Week 13
Day 1   20 minutes, including 6x1-minute
        fast, 1 minute slow
Day 2   20 minutes steady
Day 3   20 minutes, including 3x2 minutes
        fast, 2 minutes jog
Day 4   1-hour run

Week 14 – race week
Day 1   20 minutes easy
Day 2   20 minutes easy
Day 3   15 minutes easy, in race kit
Day 4   Race

Experienced runners

In time terms you will be devoting
between 4 and 6 hours to training per
week. Depending on your speed, this will
mean anything between 35 and 55 miles
per week. The schedule combines long
endurance runs with some serious quality
work, with only one in-built rest day. You
must decide as the training becomes more
intensive whether more rest days are
required. If that is the case, take them –
the key is not to get ill or injured.

Week 1
Day 1   35 minutes easy
Day 2   40–50 minutes including 8x1-minute
        fast, 2 minutes slow
Day 3   40–45 minutes steady
Day 4   40–45 minutes, including 2x5
        minutes fast, 5 minutes jog
Day 5   Rest
Day 6   35–45 minutes off-road
Day 7   60–70 minutes steady, no pressure

Week 2
Day 1   35 minutes easy
Day 2   40–45 minutes, including 6–8 fast
        bursts of 30 seconds each
Day 3   40–45 minutes steady with a brisk
        finish
Day 4   20 minutes easy, 15 minutes brisk,
        10 minutes easy
Day 5   Rest
Day 6   30 minutes easy (if racing tomorrow)

or 10 minutes slow, 10 fast, 10 slow
Day 7   10K or 10M race, or 75–85 minutes
        no pressure

Week 3
Day 1   35 minutes easy
Day 2   40–45 minutes, including
        10x1-minute fast, 2 minutes slow
Day 3   40–45 minutes steady
Day 4   45–50 minutes, including
        8x1-minute fast, 90 seconds slow
Day 5   Rest
Day 6   15 minutes easy, then timed 2M at
        planned marathon pace, then
        10 minutes jog
Day 7   80–100 minutes slow

Week 4
Day 1   35 minutes easy, off-road if possible
Day 2   Warm up, then 3–4x5 minutes fast
        (with 3-minute recovery jogs), then
        cool down
Day 3   35–45 minutes steady
Day 4   10–15x400 fast, with
        60–90-second recovery jogs
Day 5   Rest
Day 6   20–40 minutes easy
Day 7   10M or half-marathon, or 70–90
        minutes, including 30 minutes brisk

Week 5
Day 1   30–40 minutes easy
Day 2   Hills: warm up then 6–8x90 seconds
        uphill with jog recoveries
Day 3   35–45 minutes steady
Day 4   6–8x800m fast, with 2-minute
        recovery jogs
Day 5   Rest
Day 6   20 minutes easy including
        6x100m strides
Day 7   90–105 minutes slow

Week 6
Day 1   30–40 minutes easy
Day 2   35–45 minutes easy, including
        6 bursts of 150–200m fast
Day 3   40–50 minutes steady
Day 4   10 minutes easy, 15–20 minutes
        fast, 5 minutes easy

Day 5 30 minutes easy, including a few strides
Day 6 Rest
Day 7 Half-marathon race

Week 7
Day 1 30–40 minutes easy, off-road if possible
Day 2 35–45 minutes easy fartlek
Day 3 Hills: Warm up then 10–15x30–40 seconds uphill with jog recovery
Day 4 35–45 minutes steady
Day 5 Rest
Day 6 2–3x10 minutes fast with 5-minute recovery jogs, plus 1x5 minutes fast
Day 7 120 minutes easy, practise drinking on the run

Week 8
Day 1 30 minutes easy
Day 2 10–15x400m fast, with 60–90-second recovery jogs
Day 3 40–50 minutes steady
Day 4 5–8x3 minutes fast, 2 minutes jog
Day 5 Rest
Day 6 20–40 minutes depending if race tomorrow
Day 7 10K or half-marathon race, or 75–90 minutes steady

Week 9
Day 1 30–40 minutes, off-road if possible
Day 2 40–50 minutes fartlek
Day 3 40–50 minutes, including 20–30 minutes at threshold pace in middle
Day 4 30–45 minutes easy
Day 5 Rest
Day 6 30–40 minutes steady
Day 7 120–135 minutes slow

Week 10
Day 1 20–30 minutes easy
Day 2 40–50 minutes steady
Day 3 Hills: 6–8x90 seconds uphill with jog down to recover
Day 4 40–50 minutes fartlek
Day 5 Rest
Day 6 20–30 minutes jog, with 1M at race pace

Day 7 Half-marathon race

Week 11
Day 1 30–40 minutes easy
Day 2 30–45 minutes steady
Day 3 Warm up, then 3x10 minutes fast with 5-minute recoveries
Day 4 40–50 minutes steady
Day 5 Rest
Day 6 5–10 minutes easy, then 20 minutes brisk, 5 minutes jog
Day 7 135–150 minutes – should be over 20M, take drinks

Week 12
Day 1 Rest
Day 2 30–45 minutes, start slowly, finish faster
Day 3 Warm up, then 4x5 minutes fast, with 3-minute jog recoveries
Day 4 40–50 minutes fartlek
Day 5 Rest
Day 6 30 minutes easy, including a few strides
Day 7 Half-marathon race

Week 13
Day 1 30–40 minutes easy
Day 2 40–60 minutes brisk
Day 3 20–30 minutes steady
Day 4 Hills: 12–16x30–40 seconds uphill, long warm-up and cool-down
Day 5 Rest
Day 6 Warm up, 2M steady, cool down
Day 7 60–80 minutes at faster than marathon pace

Week 14
Day 1 30 minutes easy
Day 2 25–35 minutes, including 15–20 fast
Day 3 30 minutes easy, including 6x200 fast strides
Day 4 Rest or 20 minutes easy
Day 5 Rest or 20 minutes jog, in racing kit
Day 6 Warm up, 1M at race pace, cool down
Day 7 Race day

Elite schedule

This schedule is for runners who really want to commit to a serious marathon preparation. It includes some twice-a-day training, and more runs of around two hours than the previous schedule. The hard sessions should be hard, but you have to decide how hard to push yourself in the steady runs. Again, the aim is to avoid getting ill or injured, so if in doubt ease off.

Week 1
Day 1   a.m. 30 minutes easy; p.m. 30 minutes steady
Day 2   Warm up, then 4x1M reps with 3-minute recoveries
Day 3   a.m. 30 minutes easy; p.m. 30 minutes steady
Day 4   Hills: warm up, then 10–12x 40 seconds uphill, cool down
Day 5   30 minutes easy
Day 6   45 minutes easy fartlek
Day 7   80–90 minutes slow

Week 2
Day 1   a.m. 30 minutes easy; p.m. 45 minutes steady
Day 2   Warm up, then 8x1000m at 10K pace, with 2-minute recoveries
Day 3   a.m. 30 minutes easy; p.m. 45 minutes easy
Day 4   Timed fartlek: 6x2 minutes fast; 1 minute slow; 6x1-minute fast; 1 minute slow
Day 5   30 minutes easy
Day 6   30 minutes easy
Day 7   10K or 10M race, with long warm-up and cool-down

Week 3
Day 1   a.m. 30 minutes easy; p.m. 40 minutes steady
Day 2   50–60 minutes fartlek
Day 3   Warm up, then 15, 10, 5 minutes fast with 5-minute recoveries
Day 4   40 minutes easy, with 8x100m strides on grass

Day 5   30 minutes easy
Day 6   30 minutes easy
Day 7   120 minutes easy

Week 4
Day 1   a.m. 30 minutes easy; p.m. 40 minutes easy
Day 2   16–20x400m, or 20–24x1-minute fast, with 1-minute slow jog recoveries
Day 3   a.m. 30 minutes easy; p.m. 45 minutes steady
Day 4   Warm up, then 6x2 minutes uphill, warm down
Day 5   30 minutes easy
Day 6   30–50 minutes, depending on tomorrow
Day 7   10M race, or 90 minutes steady

Week 5
Day 1   a.m. 30 minutes easy; p.m. 30 minutes easy
Day 2   Warm up, then 5x1M with 3-minute recoveries, warm down
Day 3   a.m. 30 minutes easy; p.m. 40–50 minutes easy
Day 4   60–70 minutes steady
Day 5   30 minutes easy
Day 6   30–40 minutes easy
Day 7   120–140 minutes slow

Week 6
Day 1   a.m. 30 minutes easy; p.m. 30 minutes easy
Day 2   a.m. 30 minutes easy (optional); p.m. 60–70 minutes start slow, finish faster
Day 3   a.m. 30 minutes easy; pm. 40–50 minutes steady, including 8x100m strides
Day 4   Warm up, then 8x800m with 2-minute recoveries, then warm down
Day 5   30 minutes easy
Day 6   30–50 minutes easy, depending on tomorrow
Day 7   Half-marathon race, or 90 minutes steady

Week 7
Day 1   a.m. 30 minutes easy;

p.m. 45–55 minutes steady
Day 2   a.m. 30 minutes easy (optional);
        p.m. 50–60 minutes fartlek
Day 3   a.m. 30 minutes easy;
        p.m. 40–50 minutes steady, including
        8x100m strides
Day 4   Warm up, then 15, 10, 5 minutes
        fast, with 5-minute recoveries
Day 5   30 minutes easy
Day 6   40–60 minutes steady
Day 7   120–165 minutes, practise taking
        drinks

Week 8
Day 1   30–40 minutes easy, off-road if
        possible
Day 2   40–50 minutes steady
Day 3   Warm up, then 12x600m, with
        90-second recovery jogs
Day 4   60 minutes steady
Day 5   30 minutes easy
Day 6   40–50 minutes easy fartlek
Day 7   Half-marathon race, or 90 minutes
        steady

Week 9
Day 1   a.m. 30 minutes easy;
        p.m. 40–55 minutes steady
Day 2   8x90 seconds – 2 minutes uphill,
        jog back down to recover
Day 3   a.m. 30 minutes easy;
        p.m. 45–60 minutes steady
Day 4   60–70 minutes steady
Day 5   30 minutes easy
Day 6   10 minutes easy, then 15–20 minutes
        brisk, then 10 minutes easy
Day 7   120–150 minutes, take drinks

Week 10
Day 1   a.m. 30 minutes easy;
        p.m. 30–40 minutes easy
Day 2   a.m. 30 minutes easy;
        p.m. 50–60 minutes steady, including
        some faster surges
Day 3   a.m. 30 minutes easy;
        p.m. 5x1M, with 3-minute recoveries
Day 4   50–60 minutes steady
Day 5   30 minutes easy

Day 6   60–70 minutes including 10–15x
        1-minute fast, 1-minute slow
Day 7   Warm up, then half-marathon race or
        90 minutes steady

Week 11
Day 1   a.m. 30 minutes easy,
        p.m. 50–60 minutes steady
Day 2   75–80 minutes steady
Day 3   a.m. 30 minutes easy;
        p.m. 8x90 seconds – 2 minutes
        uphill, with jog-down recoveries
Day 4   a.m. 30 minutes easy,
        p.m. 50–60 minutes steady, plus
        8x150m fast strides
Day 5   30 minutes easy
Day 6   10 minutes easy, 20 minutes brisk,
        10 minutes easy
Day 7   120–140 minutes at marathon speed

Week 12
Day 1   30 minutes easy;
        p.m. 40–50 minutes steady, start
        slowly finish faster
Day 2   a.m. 30 minutes easy;
        p.m. 50–60 minutes fartlek
Day 3   a.m. 30 minutes easy;
        p.m. 8x1,000m fast, with 2-minute
        recoveries
Day 4   75 minutes steady
Day 5   30 minutes easy
Day 6   40 minutes easy, including 6x200m
        strides
Day 7   10M or half-marathon race, with
        extra running to total 16–18 miles

Week 13
Day 1   a.m. 30 minutes easy;
        p.m. 45–50 minutes steady, starting
        slowly
Day 2   Warm up, then 4x1M fast, with
        3-minute recoveries
Day 3   a.m. 30 minutes easy;
        p.m. 40–50 minutes easy, including
        a few surges
Day 4   50–60 minutes, including 2x3M
        steady
Day 5   30 minutes easy

Day 6   Warm up, then 20 minutes brisk, then cool down
Day 7   60–70 minutes at faster than marathon pace

Week 14
Day 1   40 minutes steady, including 6x150m fast strides
Day 2   Warm up, then 2M at race pace, then cool down
Day 3   30 minute easy
Day 4   20 minutes easy
Day 5   Rest or 20 minutes easy
Day 6   30 minutes jogging in racing kit
Day 7   Race day

The final week

If training has gone well, and your target race is a week away, then this is the time to make sure that all your hard work does not go to waste. You've done the main thing – prepare your body for the rigours of 26.2 miles – but there are still plenty of things that could go wrong if you're not careful. Assess realistically that you *are* fit to run. If you have a temperature, or are taking antibiotics, or have suffered an injury recently, don't do it. Even though you may have training partners, or a charity, depending on you, it's not worth the risk in these cases.

If you haven't put in the miles in training, now is not the time. Rest, rather than training is going to be of more use, although if you really are ill-prepared you should be ready for an uncomfortable and painful experience. If you are well-prepared use the final days for a couple of jogs of no more than 4 miles, with at least one in the kit that you're planning to wear during the race.

Don't wear new shoes for the race, or kit that you haven't worn before. Seams that chafe will come back to haunt you at 20 miles.

Don't try any new foods or drinks in the days before, and if you're planning to take anything other than water on board during the race, make sure you've experimented during training.

As your training tapers down your carbohydrate intake should increase. The full 'bleed-out' diet popular 20 years ago (when you starve yourself of carbohydrates until four days before the race, then load up) is not advisable; far better just to gradually increase your carbohydrate intake to 500–600g per day (roughly 70 per cent of your total food intake). Watch what you eat on the day before the race – too much fruit could give you diarrhoea. Try not to have a heavy meal in the evening as you may still feel bloated the following day. Keep drinking, preferably water, and avoid caffeine or alcohol, both of which are

Race day checklist

1. Race number
2. Safety pins
3. Race vest or T-shirt (pin your number on before you set off)
4. Shorts
5. Socks
6. Shoes
7. Petroleum jelly (for nipples and inner thighs, not feet)
8. Plasters/dressing for feet
9. Medical supports or other medication you may need
10. 500ml bottle of water
11. Snack for travelling to race
12. Old T-shirt or bin liner (to wear and discard at start)
13. Toilet paper
14. Wristwatch
15. Waterproof top and bottoms for before start
16. Clothes to change into at finish
17. Post-race snack
18. Loose change for bus fare or phone call
19. Travel documents to get away at finish if necessary
20. Towel

The marathon takes a toll but, like the medal, the memory lasts a lifetime.

diuretics – they make you go to the loo and could leave you dehydrated.

Make sure that you have prepared your kit bag (see panel, p. 62) and that you are sure of the travel arrangements to the start.

Race day

Your breakfast should be light and not bulky – toast, jam, cereal, dried fruit, or whatever you've found works for you in the past. It's a good idea to have practised your race-day routine during training before a long run.

Get to the start early, especially if there are many thousands of other runners trying to do the same thing. Be prepared for a long wait – in New York for example, you may well find yourself with three hours to kill before you start running. Try to relax, keep drinking, empty your bowels, and lie down as much as possible.

When the gun goes, aim to reach 10 miles at a pace no faster than your predicted time. if you're just looking to finish, don't worry about time – it's far more important for you not to start too fast. Build in to your plan the fact that in a major marathon, your first few miles will be slower than your desired pace. If you feel good at halfway, you can always speed up slightly and run a 'negative split' where the second half is faster than the first. If you feel a sharp pain anywhere, especially in the chest, stop running. A muscle pull or tear feels the same as cramp – massage the area and try to walk then jog. If you get a stitch, try to walk it off. Some people find that breathing out as the foot on the opposite side of the stitch hits the ground, while grunting hard, is a good remedy (it relieves the pressure on your diaphragm, and terrifies fellow runners!).

Keep drinking during the race, and you should have been doing so right up to the start – once you start running blood flow to the kidneys is reduced, so reducing the flow of urine. For most runners water is sufficient, and you may take plenty of fluid on board, especially in hot weather. If you find you are simply

Marathon splits

If you're looking to finish in a particular time, you should be looking for the following 'split' times:

To break 2:30
5:43 per mile (17:45 per 5K)
Splits
5M 28:35
10M 57:10
Half 1:15:00
15M 1:25:45
20M: 1:54:20
25M 2:22:55

To break 2:45
6:17 per mile (19:30 per 5K)
Splits
5M 31:35

10M 1:03:10
Half 1:22:30
15M 1:34:45
20M 2:06:20
25M 2:37:55

To break 3:00
6:51 per mile (21:17 per 5K)
Splits
5M 34:15
10M 1:08:30
Half 1:30:00
15M 1:42:45
20M 2:17:00
25M 2:51:15

To break 3:30
8:00 per mile (24:51 per 5K)

Splits
5M 40:00
10M 1:20:00
Half 1:45:00
15M 2:00:00
20M 2:40:00
25M 3:20:00

To break 4:00
9:00 per mile (28:00 per 5K)
Splits
5M 45:00
10M 1:30:00
Half 2:00:00
15M 2:15:00
20M 3:00:00
25M 3:45:00

---

running out of fuel, then a carbohydrate drink may help, or carbohydrate semi-solid 'goo' that is becoming popular, but it would be unwise to try either for the first time during the race.

Keep thinking positively during the run, visualise the finish or your favourite training route if you go through a bad patch. Or link up with other runners going at the same pace – this is the true camaraderie of running. Tell yourself how much training you have put in, and do not allow yourself to be defeated by the distance.

After the race

You've done it! You feel awful, but you made it. Get to the baggage bus as soon as you can to change into clean and dry clothes. Drink even if you don't feel thirsty. Keep moving – don't collapse in a heap even though this may seem very tempting. Use self-massage if you cramp up, or make use of the masseurs (if available) or first-aid teams at the finish.

Replenish your body: eat extra carbohydrates in the 'window' period, when your body is extra-receptive to carbs, 30–60 minutes after you've finished running.

Rest for a full week after the marathon. Do not run. Studies have shown conclusively that complete rest means faster recuperation. A rule of thumb is to take it easy in training for one day for every mile of the race – so, after a marathon, for the best part of a month. Do not plan realistically to run more than two marathons a year.

Be nice to yourself – rest, have a massage, take in fluids (not too much alcohol) and eat high-carbohydrate and high-protein foods.

When you do resume training – and you *will!* – just run comfortably to get back into it. Don't set yourself any goals immediately.

Training for ultras, cross-country, fells and orienteering

Ultra – beyond the marathon

You cross the marathon finish line and still feel good. You couldn't have run any faster, but you could have just kept on going. If this sounds familiar you're a prime candidate for ultra running.

Ultra running is the ultimate endurance test where the only limit is your imagination. Some ultra runs are well known and best times recorded – Land's End to John O'Groats, for example, an 870-mile trek which is often run as part of a charity fund-raising effort. Or they are simply distances covered – the west coast of America to the east, for example – purely as a personal goal.

Of course, you can run ultras competitively. There are elite events over a variety of distances – from 100 kilometres right up to multi-day races. Some races are within the scope of the regular marathoner. The Comrades Marathon in South Africa, a distance of about 96 kilometres (over twice marathon distance) attracts 11,000 runners each year, and is increasingly an international event. The Two Oceans race in Cape Town every March is even closer to the 42.2-kilometre distance, at 56 kilometres. Closer to home the London-to-Brighton run has over the years attracted marathoners and ultra-marathoners in equal measure.

The Comrades Marathon – the world's most popular 'Ultra'.

Training

Whatever attracts you to ultra running, the key factor is durability – time on your feet during training. It really is a question of quantity rather than quality, but only up to a certain point. Even in preparation for a multi-day race, mega-training mileage will only leave you feeling tired and unable to cope with the demands of the event.

Don Ritchie, multi-world record holder and possibly the best ultra runner of all time, has definite views that there is no best way to train: 'There is no "right" way to train, and success has been achieved by many different combinations of methods'. Through trial and error, Ritchie found that his weekly mileage could be anything between 20 and 160 miles!

But one of the interesting results from a study of many of the world's top ultra runners is that the optimum weekly mileage is somewhere between 100 and 120 – not that far removed from that of top marathoners.

The build-up to ultra training should follow the same pattern as regular training: the central element is the long run, usually done at the weekend. However, this is not usually of a distance longer than the planned event and recuperation during the week is a major factor. Not surprisingly, many top ultra runners have Monday planned in their diaries as an easy day. Distance is important, but it is really only trial and error which will tell you how far you should be training. Bruce Fordyce, the South African who won the Comrades six times during the 1980s, never ran over 40 miles at one go in training. Most of his long runs were between 18–25 miles, or 25–35 miles, and his weekly training would incorporate both speedwork and hill repetitions.

Speedwork seems something of a paradox when talking about endurance running; nevertheless, both Fordyce and Ritchie are perfect examples of just how important it is. Just running further at a slow pace is not enough. Indeed research shows that even for long ultras up to 600 miles, some quality work must be done for optimum performance.

Nutrition

Research among marathon runners has shown that the body runs out of fuel after about 20 miles, and that the way to counter this depleted state is by loading on carbohydrates before the run, and taking in fluids and more carbohydrates immediately afterwards. Unless you plan to be on the road for several hours or more, you probably won't need to eat.

However, Erik Seedhouse, one of Britain's top ultra runners, believes that all nutritional principles go out of the

10 diet tips for ultras

1. Eat what you can rather than what you are supposed to.
2. Eat little and often – don't wait until you are hungry.
3. After you have eaten, walk or stop – it's better for your digestion.
4. If you can stomach liquid carbo drinks, use them – it's the best way to consume large quantities of fuel.
5. Drink when you eat – the food goes down more easily.
6. Drink anyway independently of eating!
7. Try to eat when conditions are cool – food is more difficult to consume in hot weather.
8. Carbo-load as for any long-distance event.
9. Cola or lemonade can be a great lift, especially when drunk in the last two hours of a race.
10. Accept some stomach problems – they are part of the challenge.

A keen sense of balance is an asset for any cross-country runner!

window during ultra runs: 'The problem is not what you eat, but whether you can eat it. You have to follow your cravings because nothing else will go down. And you have to get something down if you want to carry on.

In an ultra race over a certain distance – and really you are not going to know what that distance is until you try it – you *will* run out of fuel, and need to eat if you want to keep going.

Eleanor Adams-Robinson, probably the greatest female ultra runner ever, tries to get to 100 kilometres on fluids alone, but beyond that she has to eat solids: 'The last thing you feel like doing is eating but you just have to force it down.'

In the longer races, stopping to eat is quite common, and you have to experiment with a variety of foods and see which enables you to carry on in the shortest possible time. Often, timing food intake to coincide with a rest period means that digestion has occurred before it's time to move on. But stomach disorders are very common in ultra running.

Cross-country, trail and fell running

If you asked athletics journalists which is the hardest race in the world to win, a fair number would say the World Cross Country Championships. At this elite event each year top track athletes meet road runners and off-road specialists over a course that demands speed and strength.

Runners in the UK have traditionally enjoyed healthy cross-country competition at club level, and this continues around the country with many successful local cross-country leagues.

But cross-country or off-road running can be of great benefit as a training aid, even if all of your racing is done on the roads. Not only does a change from pounding out the miles on Tarmac give your joints a rest, the particular demands of training off-road will only make you a better and stronger runner.

Many road runners can get obsessed with timing each run, and also tend to choose the flattest course in training. Neither is possible off-road, where the best principle is to head off and enjoy the experience, leaving your watch at home. Head for parks, canal paths and disused railway tracks as an alternative to hills, but hills will feature prominently and you must learn to take them in your stride.

Specific hill sessions mean a different training session from a steady run over a hilly course. Find a gentle gradient of around 200 metres in length and work up from one set of eight repetitions, to 1 x 10, 2 x 6, up to 2 x 8. At the end of each effort jog back down for recovery, and during the effort concentrate on your form – try to drive with the arms, lift up your knees and control your breathing.

The undulating terrain will mean that your body has to cope with a variety of conditions and efforts, similar in fact to what happens during a race when you may not be the one controlling the pace.

If you enjoy cross-country racing, rather than just training off-road, it could be that you should try fell running. Here

A hill race won't give you the gentle recoveries you enjoy in training.

again, there is a tradition of competition which has somewhat deliberately steered clear of the running boom. Fell running demands a combination of extreme fitness and complete fearlessness – the down section of any fell race can be truly terrifying for those not prepared to commit 100 per cent to the descent.

Trail running as a competitive sport has recently been officially accepted by the British Athletics Federation. Trail runs are basically off-road ultras – the South Downs Way is a favoured route – and there are many races abroad which offer a combination of extreme length and spectacular scenery.

Hashing

If the social aspect of running is almost as important as the physical activity, hashing may be a good compromise. With a very British ex-pat pedigree – the first club, the original Hash House was set up in Malaysia in 1938 – hashing is well established, with over 1,000 clubs worldwide.

Hashing is a mix between a paperchase and a trail run: one runner (the hare) devises an interesting route through the chosen area, which he marks using materials like chalk and flour. The other runners (the pack) have to follow the trails, some of which may be false.

Hashing is above all a social activity, with no real element of competition, although a regular hash will comprise runners of all standards.

Orienteering

A mixture of running and map-reading, orienteering taxes the brain as well as the muscles. In fact, your brain must be in gear before you set out, unless you want to spend a lot of time retracing your steps. The aim is to choose your own

An orienteer needs a quick mind as well as fast feet.

route to a series of checkpoints in a given order, moving between them as quickly as possible.

You are not racing head-to-head with other competitors, but are sent out at one-minute intervals, the results being decided on time.

The checkpoints, called 'controls', are marked by orange and white flags with a punch attached. When you reach the control, you punch your 'control card' to prove you've been there.

Most events offer courses of different standards, and novices can expect a route of between 4 and 6 kilometres.

Most regular runners will be fit enough; it's the map-reading that may well be the problem.

Advanced training

However long you've been running, sooner or later you'll hit a plateau – a point where you stop improving and those race times refuse to come down any further. This isn't necessarily a problem if you're running for fun and fitness, but more competitive people will become frustrated when their progress grinds to a halt. In this chapter we suggest eight ways to give yourself the extra boost that will help you to cross the plateau and reach the new heights that lie on the other side. Of course, they aren't all suitable for every kind of runner, and we've noted that where appropriate. This isn't a checklist to work through systematically – but one of these ideas might just add a new dimension to your running.

Altitude training (only for distance runners)

The theory of training at altitude (generally taken to mean any place more than 5,000ft above sea level) is simple. When you breathe, your red blood cells pick up oxygen from your lungs and transport it to your muscles. However, the amount of oxygen in the atmosphere declines progressively with altitude above sea level, making any physical exertion tougher. If you're walking, you can breathe harder, so that you take in more oxygen per minute, but it's difficult to get enough if you're running. In response to this stress, your body produces extra red blood cells so that it can capture and transport more oxygen. This means that when you return to sea level you have

extra oxygen-carrying capacity in a situation where there is no shortage of oxygen, so running becomes easier. You'll also find that you can train harder, thus increasing the benefits.

However, you won't get these benefits from a long weekend in the hills. A period of three or four weeks is ideal, giving you time to acclimatise before the really hard work begins. Take it fairly easy for the first five days and then gradually increase the effort. The toughest sessions at altitude are speed-endurance ones (fast 1,000m reps, for example), and you'll need longer recoveries than you would at sea level. To get the most out of altitude training you should eat, drink and sleep more than you would normally. Your body will also need extra iron to help it to manufacture new red blood cells, so take iron tablets. When you return from altitude (having eased off towards the end), you should be able to race well for the next couple of days. There may be a lull as your body readjusts, but then the improvement will kick in: most athletes find that the optimum time to race is two to three weeks after returning from the mountains.

Coaching

Particularly at the higher levels of the sport, there's only so much you can achieve on your own. Here, the old adage that two heads are better than one comes into its own: access to the knowledge and experience a coach can provide is invaluable. The coach's main role is to devise and develop a training and racing programme suited to the needs of the individual runner. But as often as the coach is urging you to give that little bit extra, they will be holding you back. Indeed, the more enthusiastic a runner you are, the more important it is to have someone who can look objectively at your training and warn you of the dangers of overdoing it.

The coach is also a motivator. When you're feeling low after an injury or a bad race, the coach can pick you up and help you to put things into perspective. By the same token, their job is also to bring you back down to earth if you get carried away. A good coach won't necessarily have competed at the very highest level, but they will have enough experience of running for them to know what the athlete is going through. The easiest place to find one is through a running or athletics club (few coaches work independently). Alternatively, ask other runners for recommendations.

Flexibility

Bounding, plyometrics, dynamic flexibility – there are several names for the principle that by making yourself stronger and more supple, you will enable yourself to run faster. This is particularly true of distance runners, whose stride tends to shorten as they train over longer distances. As a result, the hamstrings, quadriceps, calves and shins become tight, gradually reducing the range of motion available. By working to improve your flexibility, you can develop a long, free-flowing stride which is more efficient at fast paces.

The best time to perform flexibility exercises is in warm weather (when there's less risk of damaging the muscles), on an easy day in your training schedule. Find a strip of grass or some other soft

surface (the straight of a running track, for example) which is about 50–75m long, and perform three or four repetitions of each exercise – as with all training, build up the frequency and intensity over time. There are many exercises which come under this heading, but these are some of the most common:

Bounding
An elongated running action with exaggerated knee lift and arm swing, rather like the hop phase of the triple jump.

Knee lifts
Similar to bounding, but with a much shorter stride. You should almost be running on the spot, lifting your knees high and landing on the balls of your feet.

Skipping for height
Once again, the emphasis is on knee lift. Push off on one foot and land on the same one before bringing the front foot down. It may take practice to get the coordination right.

Skipping for distance
As above, but stressing stride length rather than height.

Bottom kicks
As with knee lifts, you're almost running on the spot, but this time kicking up your heels so that they touch your backside.

Fast feet
Similar to knee lifts again, but this time trying to move your feet as fast as possible – think of the running style of American sprinter Michael Johnson.

Mental preparation

Many books have been written on the psychology of running. However perfect your training for the big race, it can be undermined if your mental preparation isn't comparably thorough: the great runners distinguish themselves from the merely good by their ability to perform at their peak when it really matters.

In short if you're serious about becoming a better runner, you need to train your mind as well as your body. And it really is a question of training. Take the issue of self-belief. It's easy to say that if you believe you can win, you will – but much harder to put into practice. You need to acquire self-belief in stages: for example, by setting yourself a series of targets in order to build up a record of achievement that you can use to bolster yourself when the going gets tough.

Here are five things to think about – aspects of mental preparation which could help to make the difference between winning and losing:

Positive thinking

Closely related to self-belief. At the most basic level it means saying to yourself 'I can', rather than 'I can't', whether it's a question of running a certain distance or of beating a particular time or opponent. If you fail, reformulate your goals to move them back within reach.

Reliving past glories

When you're hurting, think back to a time when everything went right: when you were running smoothly, feeling superhuman. Because memories are attached to emotions, the recollection should increase your power and confidence as you tap into the way you felt on your best day.

Visualisation

While training, imagine the perfect outcome of all your hard work: you're moving through the field in the race,

coming down the finishing straight to finish first in a sensational time. This should make the training easier to bear, and aid your positive thinking on race day itself.

Coping with failure

'Whatever does not destroy me makes me stronger' – it's a valuable idea to bear in mind. In any field of endeavour, the ability to learn from mistakes distinguishes the best from the also-rans. Develop the capacity to accept the occasional mistake or failure as an opportunity for improvement.

Fantasy

Many runners find that it helps to conjure up a powerful animal – a greyhound or a cheetah. Picture your body as an engine, well greased and perfectly tuned; or pretend you're surging into the lead on the last lap of the Olympic final, cheered on by ecstatic crowds. The point is that different things work for different people, so experiment – and prepare to be surprised!

Overdistance training (especially for distance runners)

This term originally referred to the practice of running further than your target race distance in any one training session. Clearly, sprinters do this almost all the time, but the longer the race distance, the less frequent this becomes. Marathon runners, for example, rarely do individual training runs of over 20 miles.

In practice, overdistance training means raising your mileage beyond the norm in the quest for greater stamina and fitness. British 10,000m star David Bedford regularly ran 200 miles a week at his peak and, more recently, the Chinese women who took the 1993 World Championships by storm were reported to be running a marathon a day at their training camp.

Could this work for you? Unfortunately there's only one way to find out, and it's a tough one. To an extent, you can keep increasing your training mileage indefinitely, providing you take great care with your diet and recovery. As a rough guide, an extra 30 minutes of running per day should be balanced with 20–30 minutes of additional sleep and an extra 300–400 calories of nutritious food.

Above all, use fatigue as your guide: if you're tired when you start running, you need more rest. Ignore this warning sign at your peril – injury is sure to follow, and all your hard work will be wasted. Remember, the physical benefits of training actually occur during *recovery*.

Physiological testing

The days when the only way to monitor your fitness was to take your pulse are long gone. Sports physiologists have developed a range of tests which enable them to monitor your progress and trace weaknesses which might be holding you back. This isn't a straightforward process, or a cheap one. Once you've found a suitable laboratory (they're often attached to university medical schools), you'll have to pay upwards of £50 per session. Moreover, the benefits of physiological analysis are only seen over a number of tests, as trends become apparent and performance varies. Nevertheless, the information you gain from lab testing is valuable, and may give you the key to unlock the door that was barring your progress. Here are five of the most common tests:

Testing leg strength will help to identify any muscle imbalances.

VO₂max

Your maximal aerobic capacity is a good indicator of overall fitness and running performance. In a lab, VO_2max is tested by putting the runner on a treadmill and having them breathe through a valve into collecting bags. The air collected at various running speeds is analysed to determine the oxygen cost involved.

Heart-rate monitoring

Many runners now own heart-rate monitors to enable them to track their fitness. In a lab, heart rate is tested on a treadmill using an electrocardiogram (ECG).

Blood haemoglobin

Tested by taking a blood sample. The balance of red and white cells in the blood is a good indicator of general health: imbalance can be a sign of problems such as anaemia or dehydration.

Leg strength

Using the kind of leg-extension machine found in most gyms, scientists measure

the overall strength of a runner's legs and the ratio between quadricep and hamstring strength, and detect any imbalances between left and right leg.

Blood lactate

Like VO_2max, a good indicator of performance. It can be tested using a heart-rate monitor or by taking blood samples after a treadmill test and measuring the amount of lactic acid present.

Resistance training (especially for sprinters)

This involves a number of variations on strength training. What they have in common is that they work on the principle that by making it harder for yourself to run, you can increase the strength and power of your leg muscles. As such, these exercises are most commonly used by sprinters, but all runners can benefit from them.

There are numerous ways of increasing resistance while you run. The simplest is to find a surface which 'gives' more than most, such as sand or muddy paths, so that your legs have to work harder to pull your feet through on each stride. Another way of achieving the same effect is to make your feet heavier. The great Czech distance runner Emil Zátopek used to train in his army boots, but if you're not in the forces, ankle weights are a suitable alternative. Don't use these too often, though, as they will distort your running action.

To achieve whole-body resistance, runners have traditionally used a car tyre on a rope, tied around the waist so that they can drag it behind them. Nowadays there are more sophisticated (and expensive) alternatives: for instance, weighted vests with a number of pockets so that you can choose exactly how

much to weight yourself down, and small parachutes which you can clip onto a belt around your waist, and which increase the wind resistance as you run.

Whichever form of resistance training you try, don't push yourself too hard; it's a tough way to run and you'll tire more quickly. Train by distance rather than time, and concentrate on shorter repetitions.

Training camps

There are several benefits of going on a training camp or running holiday. First, you're surrounded by runners and running experts, which gives you both motivation and camaraderie. Second, the mere fact of being away from home (whether your camp is in Skegness or St Tropez) provides a welcome change from your usual running routes, and possibly a change of climate too. Third, you can devote yourself entirely to your running instead of having to fit it around your daily routine. Whether the camp lasts for a long weekend or a fortnight, the idea is to do as much running as you can safely fit into the time available. An organised training camp will provide a variety of endurance running and speedwork, specific and general sessions. In order to get the most from it, you should thus ensure that you're in good shape before you arrive, and then pace yourself. There's no point in going all-out on the first couple of days if you don't last until the end of the week. You also need to remind yourself that this isn't a holiday in the conventional sense, and that it's essential to maintain a sensible food and fluid intake. A hangover won't do much for your training the morning after, and nor will a bout of food poisoning.

If you follow these guidelines, you should find that you can train more intensively than ever before – twice a day, even three times if you already do two daily sessions. Most people find that a training holiday revitalises their running, and many use it as a springboard for a big race (such as a spring marathon) or the competitive season. Bear in mind, though, that you won't see the benefits immediately. You'll need to take it fairly easy in the week after the camp, but then the effects of your increased fitness will start to show and when this happens you'll be able to train harder, and of course race faster, than before.

Heart-rate monitoring

The rate of growth in retail sales in the UK of heart-rate monitors (HRM) of over 20 per cent per year is partly due to their increasing popularity within the running fraternity. After your running shoes, a HRM could become your most essential piece of equipment towards trouble-free and effective running training. The benefit that you can reap from your HRM depends on how seriously you want to take it. At the entry level you can use it for *awareness*, but as you become more familiar with the ins and outs of the process, you will probably end up using it for *monitoring* your training. At the sharp end of the sport, more serious runners tend to use the HRM to actually *control* their training. Do not get caught out by terminology – a heart-rate monitor and pulse monitor are and measure exactly the same thing. Armed with this information you may already know more than some shop assistants!

Product

The more advanced you become in using your HRM the more sophisticated it needs to be; so it is important that the type of monitor you buy is appropriate to your personal requirements. There is a wide number of makes and models. In terms of quality, there is little difference between them. Nowadays all HRMs consist of two components: a chest strap, which contains a transmitter, and a wristwatch, which contains the receiver. The transmitter detects the electrical activity in your heart and transmits this information, via radio telemetry, to the receiver, which calculates and displays your heart rate in beats per minute. The information is updated regularly, so every few seconds you may see minor fluctuations in the reading.

What distinguishes the various models is the range of functions on the receiver. At the entry level the receiver can just display your heart rate. However, to avoid wearing two watches, you probably want a receiver that also has a stopwatch. Another useful facility is to be able to put in alarm limits. This means that, before you workout, you can decide how you want to train. Simply put an upper and lower limit on your watch and the alarm will signal if you are running too easily, or too hard. A watch with these functions will suit most runners.

Naturally a watch can also have a standard chronograph date etc.; but the higher-level monitors might offer functions such as stopwatch splits and countdown timers (useful for interval training), data recall (so you can view your heart rates after your session) and even the facility to download all of the heart-rate information onto a PC. Naturally these extra functions start to increase the cost of the units and also require an interface and access to a computer, and for this reason they are usually considered as options that would only be contemplated by an elite runner, by a scientist or by a real enthusiast.

Awareness

You only need the most basic model to see how hard you are working when you go out running. This can be of use for two reasons. Firstly, the physiologists tell us that you can train your body harder than is actually beneficial – a strange concept but supported by research and anecdotal evidence from many runners. Seeing your heart rate on the run can let you know exactly how hard you are working as well as if you are training harder than normal. Secondly, coaches tell us that we should be using a variety of training sessions throughout the week; a mixture of longer work and shorter faster work. This running should be performed at a variety of intensities. You can check that you are doing this simply by viewing your HRM on the run. You should not be performing lung-bursting reps at the same intensity as your long steady runs, and threshold work should fit somewhere in the middle. It is a common mistake for runners to perform nearly all work at the same

A monitor will help to ensure you don't overdo things – or take it too easy.

intensity regardless of training distance.

You will probably notice that your speed for a certain heart rate is lower in the morning than it is in the evening. This is because your body is better suited to harder exercise later in the day. It is good practice to train according to your heart rate, particularly in the morning. This may make you run a little slower than you might be accustomed to, but is likely to reduce the chances of picking up niggles in the morning when running too fast without being properly warmed up and prepared.

If you wear an HRM during a race you will see that your heart rate goes higher still. This is because factors such as adrenaline start to come into play. However, using your HRM to examine your racing heart rates can be useful in trying to decipher the demands of your event, so that you know what to train for, but more about racing later.

Monitoring

The very name heart-rate monitor automatically implies that some sort of monitoring is allowed. This is where

careful use of your monitor can start to have a serious impact on the effectiveness of your running programmes. The first means of monitoring does not actually involve you running and need not even involve buying a heart-rate monitor. You can take a pulse reading at rest quite easily by feeling your radial pulse on your wrist or at the carotid on your neck. Count the number of beats in 15 seconds and multiply by 4 and you have your resting heart rate (RHR). The careful logging of this information on a daily basis can be a good indicator of your training status. However, as there are many fluctuations in heart rate throughout the day, it is important to try and standardise this measurement. Firstly try to get into the habit of making your measurement at the same time each day (usually first thing in the morning); secondly, try and make sure that your posture is the same. It does not matter whether you are sitting, lying or standing, as long as you do the same every time. Once you have taken a few measurements on successive days, you can get an idea of your baseline level. You can even plot these measurements on a chart, so that it is easy to see if there are any serious deviations from your baseline. Under such circumstances the alarm bells should be ringing.

An elevated RHR can be caused by a number of factors, such as fatigue from a race or hard training session, the onset of some sort of illness, emotional or psychological stress, or a change in environmental conditions (temperature, altitude). A good rule of thumb is that if the increase is less than 5 beats then the problem is not too severe, if between 5 and 10 then training should be modified (less intensity and volume) and if above 10 beats then a total rest day is in order. All of this, of course, is regardless of what the training schedule says, because

what you are doing here is listening to your body. If it is under pressure, for whatever reason, it makes little sense to hammer it with an eyeballs-out interval session.

Over the long term you may find that your RHR drops a little, often as you get fitter. This is because your heart can grow in size as a result of training and is able to pump more blood around your body with each beat. The net effect is that it needs to beat less times per minute to supply the same amount of blood to the areas of need and thus a drop in RHR. However, it is wrong to compare the RHR of different individuals when trying to assess fitness, because other factors are more important to running ability.

Monitoring your performance over time is a useful process, essentially to check things are going in the right direction and see that your training programme is effective. Traditionally this involved flat-out efforts in races or training, but this is not objective because conditions vary and your performance can also depend greatly on motivation. Such efforts also require disruption to your training programme, so a simple means of assessment within your training regime is advantageous. You can easily use your HRM for this provided you have alarm limits and a data recall facility. Simply plot your data on a chart after your run. It can be a long slow run, or shorter faster sessions, such as threshold work. Once you have this you have a particular window of your fitness at any one time. If you repeat the run a few weeks later and plot the data of the subsequent run on the same chart, it is easy to evaluate your fitness. If your condition has improved, you will see that if you have been running at the same pace, your heart rates throughout the run are a little lower. This shows that you have become more economical and efficient in your running. Another scenario might be where you have been using the alarm limits to keep your running at a certain intensity for optimum training effect. In this case, although the heart rates are the same throughout the run, you will find that you are actually running quicker through the run, which once again, shows an increase in efficiency and running performance.

Of course, the picture is not always rosy, you may have been injured, ill, or over-training, in which case your running performance will have deteriorated. Your heart rates at a set speed in this case are likely to be higher, or if you keep to your set heart-rate levels you will have to run slower. This is the better option and, although you might not enjoy running slower than normal, it is the safest policy, as well as useful to know where you are in terms of fitness – as opposed to wandering on kidding yourself that you are still race-fit and upsetting yourself on race day. If you are not at your best in training, there will be no one waving a magic wand on race day, so think hard as to whether racing is a sensible option when you are not quite right.

If you use your HRM all the time and stick to heart-rate limits you will, generally, notice that, if you are running the day after a hard session, your speed at your set heart rate is a little slower. This is no bad thing, because the slower speed dictated will help you to recover. Here you must be disciplined and ignore the temptation to exceed your training zone, despite the fact you may be worried that people will see you running slowly. You only get the true benefit from hard sessions when you can recover from them adequately. Running too hard the next day does not help the recovery process, so stay loyal to your HRM and it will look after you.

In extreme cases of fatigue or over-training, you may find that rather than have elevated heart rates in training, you actually struggle to raise your heart rate to the normal level, regardless of how much effort you are putting in. Once you are at this stage it is time to have a proper rest, which means nothing but easy or steady running and no interval training. Depending on the severity of your over-training and fatigue, a few days of recuperation should see you back to normal to resume your usual schedule.

Another means of using your HRM to assess your health status and how you are going is to monitor your recovery pulse. This is done simply by one of two ways: you can time how long it takes your heart rate to return to a pre-determined level after a session, say 120. Of course, this will vary according to the duration and intensity of your session, but after logging the information carefully in a diary, you can start to establish typical recovery times for certain types of session. If after a steady run you normally find it takes 30 seconds to reach 120, but one day it takes about a minute, this should be a warning, similar to that given in the RHR example. This process is particularly useful at the end of a morning run for the runner who trains twice a day. A longer recovery time should indicate an easier session is required in the evening.

The other method is to check your heart rate after a set time, say 30 seconds. If the reading is still much higher than normal, then once again you are not fully recovered and care should be taken not to overdo things.

Control

A lot of the above depends on running at the right heart rate for your different sessions. The difficulty comes in establishing what are the correct training heart rates for different training sessions in individuals. Unfortunately each runner is different; you can have different resting, training and maximal heart rates despite being the same age and fitness level, which makes pinpointing the correct levels tricky. The Italian physiologist Francesco Conconi devised a test that was popular in the 1980s in trying to pinpoint the anaerobic threshold. The test involves wearing your HRM and running at a series of speeds, increasing every 200m right up until exhaustion. At a set deflection point, the threshold was proposed to exist. In recent years this deflection point has proved to be unreliable in many subjects and is generally not well accepted as a valid test.

Another popular means of trying to set training heart rates is to use percentages of maximum heart rate. Formulae exist to help you guestimate your maximum heart rate, such as 220 minus age. However, this proves unreliable for many and should not be trusted. The safest way to establish your maximum heart rate is to wear your HRM, while you perform two hard 3-minute efforts, separated by a couple of minutes' easy jogging. Naturally this should follow a thorough warm-up. If you check your heart rate through the last minute of the second effort, this will probably equate to your maximum heart rate – higher than that found in a race or hill session. You can then use percentages of this figure to control your training sessions. The difficulty then comes in trying to pick what percentages to use.

Sport science might have the answer, when blood lactate samples are taken at a variety of training paces. The construction of a heart rate-lactate profile can be used to prescribe the correct training heart rates for each type of session that you do. Your long run should be performed at a heart rate where there is little or no lactate accumulation, while threshold work should be performed at a heart rate where the lactates are high, but stable: the maximum aerobic steady state. This should give you the optimum aerobic benefit and such sessions are most useful in improving endurance performance. The heart rate is a great means of control because, if you go too hard, you start to use a greater contribution from anaerobic metabolism and thus the impact of an aerobic session is lost. However, if you go too easy, then you are not training as hard as you can and the session is no longer optimal.

Racing

Because other factors, such as adrenaline, come into play on race day, it is not safe to use your heart rate to prescribe your pace in races. This does not mean that you should not wear your HRM in races. Race heart-rate profiles can be very useful in trying to explain good and bad races. Athletes that start off too hard and slow down progressively in races often find that the heart rate is high in the first few minutes, but such heart rates cannot be maintained. If the climatic conditions or terrain vary, then these will show up on your heart-rate trace. The information that you gain can help you plan race strategy for the future, in terms of correct pace, how hard to tackle hills etc.

Cross-training

Using other modes of exercise to enhance your aerobic potential is popular. It must be said that the best form of activity to boost your running is running, but activities such as water running and cycling are ways of maintaining fitness, without the impact associated with running. If you wear your HRM in the gym while using a bike or rowing machine, you should expect to see your heart rates much lower for a given level of effort. This does not mean that you are being lazy: because you are carrying your body weight when you are running,the heart rates are higher than in modes of exercise where the body is supported, such as rowing and cycling. Furthermore, when you are running you are exercising a greater proportion of your muscle mass than in cycling, so a greater cardiac output (amount of blood pumped in litres per minute) is required. To avoid disappointment, you should aim to use your HRM during cross-training to maintain your fitness and add variety to your workouts, rather than directly attempt to boost your running.

Cross-training for runners

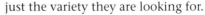

Thirty years ago, if you were a runner that was all you did. Times have changed. Ever since the first triathlons back in the 1970s, runners started to broaden their sporting horizons. Instead of making running their only exercise they're trying out activities like cycling, swimming, walking and circuits. It's not just the variety they are looking for.

Studies have shown that cross-training can have a significant positive impact upon your running by improving the overall intensity of your training.

Injuries are also a big reason for runners to switch to cross-training. The more you run and the harder you make your sessions the greater the likelihood of injury. The most common problem comes from the action of running itself, as you overuse the muscles and joints of the legs. Cross-training offers variety and a chance to put in an intense session without killing your legs. Cross-training will also make you stronger. Many cross-training activities, like cycling, stair-climbing or resistance-training, build stronger leg muscles. Running at race pace requires fewer leg-muscle cells as each is now stronger. You should therefore be able to run more efficiently and faster.

Many runners find cross-training a mental lift after the tedium of some running workouts, that is providing they can obtain the same intensity in the session. Adapting to and coping with the different exercises also improves their mental toughness for running.

Despite all the potential advantages, the subject of cross-training is a contentious one. What you should do, how long you should do it for or whether indeed you should be doing anything other than running have all been the

Low-impact cross-training is a great ally against injury.

subject of debate. There is a body of opinion, for example, which preaches the specificity theory. This contends that the only way to improve in a sport is to actually practise that sport. If you're a runner, then you should run. Anything else is a waste of time. If you are looking for a break from running, then a day off is is far better than lifting weights or doing an hour on a bike.

Such views tend to cast runners as a single body. The reality is that people run for different reasons and there are clearly groups, such as those running for fitness or those who are injured or prone to injury, who would benefit from the greater variety of training and become faster and more consistent runners. Even proponents of cross-training, however, cannot agree on exactly what you should

The ergometer proves that cross-training needn't be easy.

be doing. Some believe that runners should cross-train using exercises and activities that are as close to running as possible. The logic is that the stronger you can make your running muscles the better you will run.

The contrary view suggests that cross-training is all about resting your running muscles. That is, you should use sports which are as different from running as possible. You can then burn up calories and get a good workout while resting your running muscles. In this way you can avoid the one-sport muscle imbalances that frequently lead to injury.

The trouble is that all these different views on cross-training do have their merits. Ultimately what you decide to do will depend very much on your personal goals and the type of runner you are or want to be. The following advice is designed for a range of different runners; all you need to decide is which one you actually are.

Fitness runners

These are people who are using running as part of an all-round fitness programme.

What to do?

You should concentrate on the muscles that running neglects. The quadriceps, for example, get little work compared to the calves, buttocks and hamstrings and the upper body is a forgotten region. Running is great for the cardiovascular system but if you're concerned with total body fitness you need a much wider variety of activities. Run twice a week and do a complementary exercise, like cycling or stair-climbing, on one or two other days. In addition, 20 minutes of circuit training twice a week will help you to work any muscles you may have missed.

Which exercises?

Concentrate on those that work the upper body and quadriceps. Rowing, swimming or total body machines, like cross-country skiing machines or Health Riders, are probably the best.

Novice runners

These are people who are running under 15 miles a week and, while there are similarities with fitness runners, they are running more to build up their cardiovascular system, lose weight and improve their general physical condition.

What to do?

Concentrate on improving the cardiovascular system; a strong heart and lungs will supply more fuel to your working leg muscles, which will allow you to run more consistently without feeling out of breath. Those switching from another sport will probably be fit enough to run a few miles without much problem, but don't try to do too much

too soon. Running can be a shock to the muscles, tendons and ligaments.

The best cross-training programme is one which mixes running and other activities in equal measure. This will allow you to build your cardiovascular system and muscle strength simultaneously without risk of injury. Your body is only likely to be able to take one hard session a week so split your tougher sessions between running and cross-training.

Which exercises?

Those that strengthen as many of your running muscles as possible, as well as improving their co-ordination and teaching them to deal with storing and using fuel effectively. Cross-country skiing, stair-climbing and in-line skating will all work well. Circuit training twice a week will also help protect against running-related injuries (see pp. 85–88).

Intermediate runners

These are more serious runners doing up to 40 miles a week, with strong running and racing aspirations.

What to do?

You should already have a strong cardio-vascular system and should select intense cross-training activities that specifically target your running muscles and maintain that high level of aerobic fitness.

Your aim should be to run three times as much as you cross-train. If you are doing two hard sessions a week, select cross-training sessions that allow you to exercise at a moderate intensity. The aim is to give your running muscles an extra workout without the extra pounding. If your body can only handle one hard workout a week, adding an interval or tempo cross-training sessions will provide a boost to your running.

Quick and easy circuit

The name of this circuit speaks for itself. Simply move from one exercise to another, performing ten reps of each to make up a set. Take a minute's rest between sets, then go through them again. Perform the exercises quickly. You can enhance the endurance aspect by removing the rest between sets – each body part recovering as you work another. You can vary the reps in each set, progressing up from ten through to thirty. You'll need to reduce the pace, though, if you're not resting between sets.

Oregon circuit

This session originated in the USA and is best performed outside, placing nine exercises around a 1,000-metre circuit; exercise stations are at 100-metre intervals. After each exercise, run to the next, but allow thirty seconds' rest after exercises 3, 6 and 9. Then follow the set with a run round the whole circuit to give an aerobic training effect.

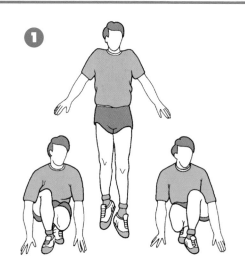

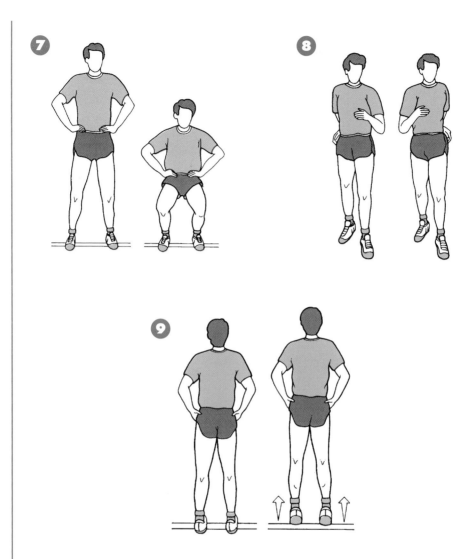

Which exercises?

To achieve a high-intensity cardiovascular workout you need to use a stationary machine in a high cadence, it will slow your turnover and keep your heart rate up. For muscle-specific workouts, try to find a cross-country skiing machine or a stationary bike.

Advanced runners

These are accomplished runners doing more than 40 miles a week. You should have maximised your cardiovascular conditioning as well as the strength, efficiency and co-ordination of your leg muscles.

What to do?

Cross-training probably won't do you much good. To improve your running, which is your primary goal, you need to do more quality runs. You should be doing at least two hard runs a week. Since both hard running and high mileage can increase your injury risk, your best bet may be rest, which will allow you to rest completely for your next session. If you don't want to rest, think about low-intensity cross-training sessions that don't tax your running muscles. This will burn calories and keep you mentally fresh. The best time to insert any cross-training into your programme is immediately after a hard day, which would usually be an easy day.

What exercises?

Anything that gives your running muscles a break, like swimming, pool-running or rowing will help you recover for the next running session. Circuits won't do you any harm either, strengthening your leg muscles so they can withstand the constant pounding on the roads.

Injury-prone runners

Two out of three runners suffer an injury every year. If you regularly average more than two running-related problems, then you are injury-prone.

What to do?

If you fall into that category then you are going to have more need of cross-training than most runners, firstly as alternative exercise while you are injured but also as a way of cutting down on the injuries themselves. Studies have shown that runners can maintain their running times for up to six weeks using cross-training alone, providing it is done at the proper intensity.

The best combination is between two

Cross-training principles

1. It's an alternative not an addition

Don't just add a cross-training session to an already rigorous running programme. Try to substitute particular sessions rather than adding, at least at the beginning. If you are logging a tough 50 miles a week, even a gentle hour of swimming could push you into an over-training zone which will detract rather than add to your running.

2. Start off slowly

Cycling, swimming or circuits will put demands on muscles that you aren't used to using. Ease into the activities and try

to build up your tolerance gradually. Injuries are often the cost of pushing too hard too quickly.

3. Avoid activities that might aggravate running injuries

Runners with foot problems are doing themselves no favours by taking up long-distance walking or hiking. Likewise if you have an Achilles problem try to avoid cycling.

4. Aim for equality of sessions

To achieve the maximum fitness benefit from cross-

training, the new session should duplicate the duration of the run it is replacing, that's of course after you feel comfortable with the activity. If you usually run for an hour in the morning and you want to cycle, do it for an hour as well.

5. Don't ignore fatigue

If you feel tired, stop. Fatigue is a warning that your body needs rest not more exercise. The whole idea behind cross-training is to keep your interest in exercise and your fitness high over the long term – not to cripple your body.

and four running sessions a week and two cross-training sessions. They should target running-specific muscles to increase their strength and efficiency without subjecting them to pounding. This rarely produces injuries since the pounding of running is usually the main culprit. Since running injuries are often the result of high-intensity sessions, limit them to one a week; if you want to add harder sessions use cross-training.

Cycling: the number one cross-training exercise for runners.

Which exercises?

Keep the exercises specific to running. Static gym exercises such as stair-climbing and cross-country skiing are good choices. If you are suffering a specific injury, like a stress fracture, then your choices are going to be limited to non-weight bearing exercises like swimming or deep-water running. Again, twice-a-week circuit training will help to strengthen muscles, tendons and ligaments.

The runner's top five

1. Cycling

This is probably the best running alternative. One study found that a combination of running and cycling in a week created the same benefits as the running-only exercise for an equal period of time. Other studies have demonstrated how cycling can add intensity to a running schedule without increasing the risk of injury.

The best sessions after a warm-up are short five-minute intervals at a pace similar to 10-kilometre intensity. Even shorter intervals of one minute hard and 30-second breaks will boost anaerobic capacity; these should be maximal efforts at 5-kilometre pace. Build up the length and intensity of intervals slowly; start with three and work up to ten.

2. Weight training

The benefit of weight or other resistance training to runners has been backed up by solid research, which shows it can make four per cent improvements in running economy and reduced heart rates. It also strengthens and improves muscles and bones against injury. Circuit training – a form of rapid-fire weight training – builds muscles and provides a decent cardiovascular workout at the same time. You should concentrate on exercises that are weight bearing, such as squats, bench-stepping and heel raises. Try to avoid exercises that put you in a seated position but insert some abdominal exercises, an area that most runners forget. Any exercise that uses the same muscles and motions as running will be of particular help as the new-found strength carries over to your running.

3. Deep-water running

This is a core activity for any injured runners looking to maintain their running fitness. Some top athletes, for example, have managed to maintain their speed with aqua running, despite a six-week break for injury. Its real benefit is that it completely mimics the action of ordinary running in a weight-free environment. It can be tedious, particularly for long sessions, but try to maintain the same intensity as you would do for a land session.

4. Stair-climbing

This stimulates the action of hills by increasing the aerobic capacity of your quadriceps. According to research, stair-climbing can keep pace with regular running for periods up to eight or nine weeks, by increasing your leg strength

and power. The downside to stair-climbing is the low stride rates, even at maximum intensity; that means you can improve your aerobic endurance but it's hard to learn to run much faster using a stair-climber. As with most static-machine exercises, try to do short-interval bursts of no more than five minutes, running at 5-kilometre pace or faster. Gradually increase the number of repetitions.

5. Cross-country skiing

This is like running, with two main differences. You don't have the hard ground-impact of running and it's a total body exercise requiring upper-body as well as lower-body strength.

Your problem is actually practising genuine cross-country skiing in the UK, but the increasing number of specialist indoor machines have opened the activity to a wider group.

One negative side is the motion itself: the gliding action of cross-country skiing is markedly different to that of running. It doesn't teach you to bounce explosively from foot to foot. But you can't fault the cardiovascular workout and you can transfer your high-level fitness to running with a couple of weeks of solid skiing.

Injury prevention

Injuries are a fact of running life. They are as much a part of the sport as long Sunday morning runs and midweek club nights. A recent study of 3,000 runners carried out by *Runner's World* magazine discovered that nearly half that number had been injured during the previous year and that the majority of the injuries had been sustained while running on paved roads and pavements.

The good news is that most common running injuries are frequently attributed to overuse and are therefore preventable – with a little understanding and care. Controlling injuries can be as simple as choosing softer running surfaces and maintaining a high level of conditioning.

It's when injuries do occur that things get complicated. Today's sports medicine for runners is more sophisticated than ever – and, perhaps, more confusing, with more terms, more therapies, more options.

This chapter is designed to guide you through the maze and offer simple, practical advice on how to recognise and treat the vast majority of injuries you are likely to encounter in your running career. It also deals with a number of more common complaints and ailments familiar to most experienced runners and offers a guide to the various basic

The golden rule for pain:
stop running, apply ice.

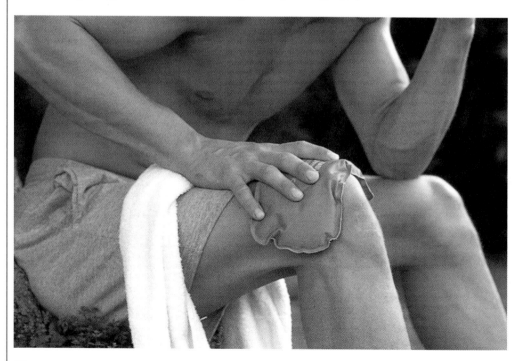

treatment options available. Finally you will also find advice on the preventive measures you can take to avoid the injury in the first place.

Of course, it is not the answer to everything. You can only go so far with words and diagrams, sometimes your best bet will be to consult a doctor immediately. No work of reference can take into account all the factors and circumstances that contribute to each individual's health.

Foot injuries

Achilles bursitis
Bursae can develop both inside and outside the Achilles tendon insertion into the calcaneum bone of the heel.
Symptoms: If there is enough friction between the shoe and your heel, these bumps may become painful.
Causes: People who have unusually bumpy heel bones, and runners who are tall and have high arches and tight

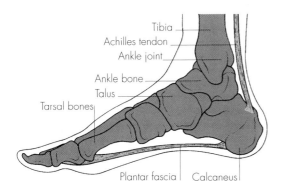

Tibia
Achilles tendon
Ankle joint
Ankle bone
Talus
Tarsal bones
Plantar fascia Calcaneus

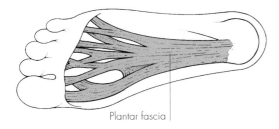

Plantar fascia

Achilles tendons, are susceptible to Achilles bursitis.
Treatment: To avoid the friction, pad the heel area of your shoes or cut the shoe away from the afflicted area; rest until the pain subsides. If all else fails, a surgeon can remove the offending piece of bone and reshape the heel.

Achilles tendinitis
Symptoms: As well as persistent pain and swelling, there may well be a grating or crackling sensation as you move the ankle to and fro. A mild, less persistent form of this may merely be Achilles tendon strain.
Causes: The major causes are overuse, change of terrain, such as running up steep hills if you're not used to it, a sudden increase in mileage, and wearing inappropriate shoes.
Treatment: Rest it and ice it. Take special care with the use of anti-inflammatory drugs, which may mask an injury and a potential complete rupture. When running is possible, a heel raise may help to reduce the amount of stretching within the tendon during training.
Prevention: Wearing shoes with good shock-absorbency is vital, and you must ensure that there is no pressure on the Achilles tendon, especially from a heel tab. Proper warming up and stretching should limit the tendency to suffer from tendinitis, and make sure you're well prepared *before* you step up your weekly mileage.

Achilles tendon rupture
Symptoms: Sudden pain, often some shock and swelling, but particularly an inability to stand on the toes of the injured foot.
Treatment: Although some physicians recommend putting the foot in plaster and allowing the ruptured ends of the tendon to join naturally, surgical repair is

usually the most successful treatment.
Prevention: Stretch regularly and conscientiously and take care of your feet and shoes. Older runners suffer more, as their tendons are less supple.

Ankle sprain

This normally involves either stretching or tearing of the ligaments on the outer side of the ankle joint, and may vary from mild to complete ligament rupture.
Symptoms: At the time of injury the pain may be very severe, then ease, then worsen again as local bleeding occurs. There may be visible bruising which tracks down towards the foot. The ankle will be unstable. Only X-rays can confirm that no fracture has occurred.
Cause: Uneven terrain, tripping or stumbling.
Treatment: Stop running immediately, as further damage can occur if you try to run on a sprain. Ice and anti-inflammatories will cure a mild sprain, but will need to be continued for longer in more serious cases. The worst sprains require total immobilisation, even though this may hamper rehabilitation, which must include strengthening of the lower-leg muscles (which limit ankle instability). Taping may be useful in early training to limit movement and avoid re-damaging the ankle, but never do this when racing.
Prevention: Good ankle mobility, and the strength gained through simple exercises (such as standing on one foot), will limit the tendency to sprains.

Blister

A collection of fluid within the outer layers of the skin.
Symptoms: The skin invariably swells and becomes sensitive to pressure, and occasionally reddened.
Causes: A blister is the result of irritation between two surfaces, such as socks or shoes and skin. The friction makes the outer and inner layers of the skin separate and fill with fluid.
Treatment: When possible, leave the blister alone for 24 hours to allow it to heal itself. If the fluid isn't re-absorbed, lance the blister as follows: sterilise a needle by heating it in a flame or boiling water. Swab the blister with disinfectant such as alcohol. Prick two holes on opposite sides of the blister and press gently on the blister with sterile gauze to push out the fluid. Do not remove the loose skin. Smear the blister with antiseptic and cover it with a sterile gauze. If the blister re-fills, lance again and soak it in Epsom salts. Many runners prefer to leave the blister open and cover it with sterile lubricated jelly or powder.
Prevention: Clean and well-fitting socks and shoes are less likely to cause friction, though careful covering of vulnerable areas prior to a run, and avoiding wetness in the shoe, will also help to limit it.

Bone spur

A benign growth extending away from a bone, often underneath the foot at the origin of the plantar fascia or at the insertion of the Achilles tendon.
Symptoms: A spur can be intensely painful, and inflammation may make it tender, hot and reddened.
Causes: Repeated stress of the bone lining pulling away from the heel bone can result in inflammation, and ultimate calcification, of the ligaments originating from the bone. A tight plantar fascia may also contribute.
Treatment: Begin applying ice and take an anti-inflammatory medication. You can relieve the pain by reducing the pull upon the bone: wearing running shoes with a rigid heel counter, and a well-cushioned midsole can also help. In the case of plantar fasciitis, an orthotic may

well reduce the 'bowstring' pull upon the heel spur.

Prevention: When you resume training, start slowly on soft, forgiving surfaces. Applying ice after each run will help to reduce discomfort. Applying gentle warmth may help in the final stages of recovery.

Bunions

Swellings on the inner side of the foot, at the joint of the big toe.

Symptoms: There is usually tenderness, pain and stiffness over the crooked joint. Chronic bunions usually overlie arthritic joints, and are very painful.

Causes: Pronation, poorly fitting shoes and family heredity are all likely culprits.

Treatment: Although most bunions eventually require surgery, it is sometimes possible to alter the foot alignment with an orthotic, re-training the muscles of the foot and using padding between the toes. Wear a doughnut pad over the bony growth to reduce friction, and if your bunion is rubbing hard against the inner surface of your shoe, make a stab incision in the shoe at the point of contact to relieve pressure. For relief from pain and inflammation, try aspirin or ibuprofen. Anyone with chronic bunions should wear running shoes when not running.

Prevention: Ensure your shoes fit, with a wide toe box, this will reduce some pressure. Orthotics or a toe-spacer made of sponge will probably help alleviate discomfort.

Callus

A thickening of the skin, usually over an area which is exposed to chronic irritation and friction during running.

Symptoms: Calluses are usually thickened and painless, providing there is no underlying bursa.

Causes: Constant friction and pressure make the skin thicken for self-protection.

Treatment: Thinning the callus by rubbing it with a pumice stone may help. Avoiding pressure by using felt pads or orthopaedic foam will allow the thickening to disperse over several months.

Prevention: Wear shoes which fit properly.

Corns

Symptoms: A hard area within the skin that is often deeper and more painful than calluses.

Causes: Tight or ill-fitting shoes are the most common cause, though it may be that the bone structure of the foot is abnormal.

Treatment: Although corns can be surgically exercised, it is often sufficient to relieve pressure with a felt pad around the corn, allowing it to soften and drop out.

Prevention: Corns will recur unless the underlying cause is discovered. Support flat longitudinal arches, get rid of tight shoes, and discuss surgery to correct chronically deformed feet.

Heel bruise

Symptoms: Pain and tenderness whenever you put weight on the heel.

Causes: Generally, a heel bruise results from stepping on a hard object such as a stone, or from running long distances on a hard surface in thin-soled shoes. It occurs because the fat pad between the skin and the bone fails to absorb the pressure of landing.

Treatment: See a doctor to distinguish this injury from other causes of heel-bone pain. Mild heel bruises will respond to rest and adequate cushioning of the heel. More severe cases may be treated with a plastic heel cup to distribute the weight-bearing forces over a wider area.

Prevention: Never run long distances on hard surfaces in light, thin-soled shoes.

Ingrowing toenail

Symptoms: This usually affects the big toe, where the nail grows into the flesh of the toe. Local swelling, inflammation, redness and pain, together with a secondary bacterial infection are common.

Causes: Abnormal nail growth may be caused by tight shoes, poor nail hygiene or trimming.

Treatment: Soaking the toe in antiseptic can help, but the best way to get rid of an ingrowing toenail is to use antibiotics to eliminate the infection and cut the nail correctly. This may include making a V-shaped nick in the centre and lifting the sides out of the flesh. If this fails, the nail may need to be surgically removed.

Prevention: Don't cut your nails too short or allow them to grow too long. Frequent cutting, wearing clean socks, and wearing shoes with a wide toe box should all prevent chronic pressure on the toenail.

Morton's toe

Symptoms: It may be symptom-less, or may produce pain as the second toe absorbs a greater amount of landing pressure. It could cause a stress fracture to the second metatarsal.

Causes: A long second metatarsal and a tendency to over-pronate.

Treatment: Orthotics can support the first metatarsal head where a long second toe exists, while a metatarsal arch support across the transverse arch may help an early neuroma. Some runners may need surgery.

Prevention: Don't ignore foot pain. Get the foot examined if the pain persists.

Plantar fasciitis

An inflammation of the fascia which runs from the heel bone to the base of the toes, and which supports the bottom of the foot.

Symptoms: Pain and local tenderness which usually begins at the heel, then radiates out into the midsection of the foot. The pain becomes acute if you put pressure on the tender area.

Causes: Although this is an overuse injury, it is most common among runners with high arches or flat feet.

Treatment: Early treatment is crucial. To complicate matters, plantar fasciitis frequently occurs along with heel spurs. Orthotics, cushioned shoes and massage with ice or a golf ball may solve the problem.

Runner's toe

A pooling of blood under the toenail.

Symptoms: A toe becomes painful and the nail becomes red or blackened.

Causes: Tight and small running shoes will constantly rub the nail and nail bed, though blisters and stubbing the toe may also cause this painful condition.

Treatment: To relieve the pressure, you need to make a hole in the nail and drain the blood. Either heat the tip of of a small straightened paper clip or a needle and use it to burn through the nail until a drop of blood comes out. The hole made by the needle will allow the old blood to drain out, and this can be gently squeezed before sterile and dry dressings are applied. The damage to the nail bed will often cause the toenail to fall off, though this may take many weeks. During this time, protect and cover the nail bed with a plaster.

Prevention: Buy shoes with more space in the toe box.

Sprain

This occurs when a ligament (which helps to hold two bones in apposition) is stretched beyond its normal limits. Any of the small ligaments or muscles joining the foot bones can be sprained or strained, as can other joints of the body.

Symptoms: There will usually be acute pain at the time of the injury, followed by tenderness and swelling.

Causes: Any abnormal stress or force on a ligament, such as a fall or running on uneven ground in unsupportive shoes, can separate the bones and cause a sprain. Sprains can range from mild to severe.

Treatment: Start icing at once, and continue until the area is painless. Localised physiotherapy can also help. If the pain persists you should see a doctor, in case it indicates a fracture or more serious damage.

Prevention: Proper warming up is important, and wearing supportive shoes may limit damage, but any runner can develop a sprain.

Stress fracture of the second metatarsal

Also known as 'march fracture' since the First World War, when many soldiers developed this injury after being required to march long distances in ill-fitting shoes. The metatarsal stress fracture commonly affects the second toe with a hairline break.

Symptoms: Pain occurs gradually in the area of the damaged bone, and it increases as you continue to exercise.

Causes: A stress fracture is an overuse injury, made worse by running on hard surfaces in shoes with insufficient cushioning. Poor biomechanics and over-tiredness increase the likelihood of injury.

Treatment: While you get a diagnosis, rest from any exercise that causes you pain. Unfortunately, a stress fracture probably won't show up on an X-ray for three to four weeks, although a bone scan will show the damage sooner. You can do any non-weight-bearing exercise (e.g. swimming or cycling), but your recovery should only include walking and running when these are pain-free.

Prevention: Wearing good shoes which absorb shock, and running on soft surfaces, will limit the opportunity for stress fractures to develop. Orthotics may also help to spread the load on landing. Also increase training loads gently.

Lower leg injuries

Compartment syndromes

These affect the rigid sheaths which contain the lower leg muscles.

Symptoms: The two posterior compartment syndromes usually produce dull, cramping pain, while those to the lateral and anterior compartments can be

Basic treatments

How to ice an injury

Cover the skin with two layers of a plastic wrap. Put ice on top of the injury and compress with a bandage of tight-fitting clothing such as a spandex of Lycra. Elevate the injury and ice it for 20 minutes, stop for 10 minutes, ice again for 20 minutes, stop for 10, ice for 20, stop for 10.

If you can manage this three times a day for three consecutive days you will receive a tremendous anti-inflammatory effect. If you don't have time for this routine, do what you can. Crushed ice, packs of frozen peas and gel packs all work well.

Heat does not have the anti-inflammatory effect that ice has, but hot tubs and heating pads may be very relaxing to your muscles and your mind. Rubs and balms applied to the skin have no healing effect: they create a mild stinging sensation in the skin and distract you from your pain.

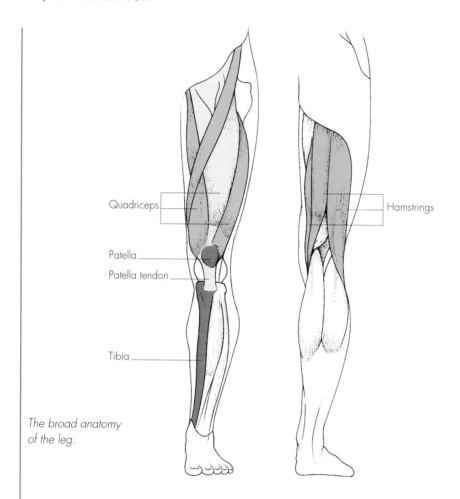

Quadriceps

Hamstrings

Patella

Patella tendon

Tibia

The broad anatomy of the leg.

acutely painful, especially to the touch. Pain will persist after you stop running, and you may feel numbness or tingling in the feet.

Causes: Compartment syndromes often affect untrained runners who cover longer distances than they're ready for. As you do more exercise, increased blood flow and secreted fluid can cause swelling within the muscle; the inelastic sheath is unable to take the pressure and becomes painful.

Treatment: RICE is important in the acute phase, and you should reduce your training. Then build up gently, and check that your shoes are appropriate for the distances you intend to run.

Periostitis

If the thin, sensitive tissue surrounding a bone is irritated, it can be called a periostitis. This occurs most commonly along the medial border of the tibia.

Symptoms: There is usually pain over a two- or three-inch length of the tibia, and there may be some roughness or swelling.

Causes: Periostitis is almost certainly caused by overuse, poor biomechanics and poor footwear.

Treatment: You need a medical assessment, which may include X-rays and a bone scan to eliminate stress fracture. Although anti-inflammatories may ease the symptoms, and some running on soft surfaces may be possible, correcting the primary cause (whether this is in your foot or your shoe) is vital to prevent periostitis recurring.

Shinsplints

A vague term describing pain in the lower leg. The pain may be caused by a stress fracture, compartment syndrome or periostitis.

Symptoms: Invariably, pain, the site depending on the cause.

Causes: Multiple, including over-pronation, over-training and shoes which fail to support the foot properly.

Treatment: Depends on the cause, though rest may be required for total healing.

Prevention: You can generally limit shinsplits if you only increase your training in gentle increments, observe shin and foot pain carefully to prevent them worsening, and seek early treatment.

Stress fracture (tibia)

Hairline fractures in the tibia typically occur at the end of the bone near the ankle, though they may also be observed elsewhere.

Symptoms: A crescendo pain, starting as a dull ache and progressing in intensity as distances increase. Typically, the pain decreases at night. The site may be tender and slightly swollen.

Causes: Stress fractures of the tibia are overuse injuries, worsened by higher-than-usual mileage or running on hard surfaces.

Treatment: If you have the symptoms, assume that the pain is caused by a stress fracture until you can prove otherwise. This will prevent a complete fracture of the bone, which would mean spending months in plaster. It is essential not to undertake any activity which is painful.

Prevention: To limit the likelihood of a stress fracture, increase your mileage

The 5 most common running injuries

1. Runner's Knee, *Chondromalacia Patellae*, (20–25 per cent of all injuries)
2. Shinsplints (15 per cent)
3. Iliotibial band friction (10 per cent)
4. Achilles tendinitis (8 per cent)
5. Plantar fasciitis (8 per cent)

(source: *Runner's World* survey)

gradually, wear shoes with good shock-absorbing qualities and run on soft surfaces.

Knee injuries

Arthritis

Symptoms: In milder cases you may suffer from no more than mild discomfort and lubrication of the joint, though exercise and movement may actually help to relieve the symptoms. In more serious cases there is pain and

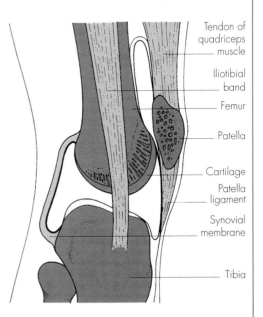

Tendon of quadriceps muscle

Iliotibial band

Femur

Patella

Cartilage

Patella ligament

Synovial membrane

Tibia

Knee pain originates either from the knee itself or its neighbouring muscles.

inflammation, which in turn causes further cartilage damage and breakdown in a vicious circle.

Causes: Damage to the cartilage within the joint, which becomes unable to repair itself, and the opposing surfaces of the joint become roughened.

Treatment: Initially, rest and anti-inflammatories. Consult a doctor early on.

Baker's cyst

An accumulation of fluid behind the knee joint, also known as a popliteal cyst.

Symptoms: Usually nothing more than a painless swelling.

Causes: A weakness of the capsule of the knee allows it to bulge and fill with synovial fluid from the knee joint. In adults, there may be local disease such as arthritis, torn cartilage or other forms of inflammation.

Treatment: Baker's cyst can only be treated once a cause is established, though many runners require no treatment at all. See a doctor if the problem persists.

Chondromalacia patellae

Also known as 'Runner's Knee', this is literally a softening of the cartilage of the patella. The back surface of the kneecap fails to run smoothly through the groove at the front of the femur. The condition may be worsened if there is an unequal pull from the quadriceps muscles.

Symptoms: These may be of two types, either a persistent ache or a sudden acute pain ('angina' of the knee) halfway through a run. The pain disappears when you are forced to stop.

Causes: Simplistically speaking, *chondromalacia patellae* is the result of a quadriceps muscle imbalance caused by performing inappropriate activity (e.g. leg extensions on a machine) or sustained damage to the knee or leg. In reality,

there are multiple causes which are not yet fully explored.

Treatment: It does no harm to perform straight-leg quadriceps exercises, preferably under the guidance of a knowledgeable doctor or physiotherapist.

Prevention: *Chondromalacia patellae* may be the result of over-pronation, or simply bad training habits (e.g. always running on one side of the road) or simply your shoes. Analysis by an expert should help to locate the cause.

Iliotibial band syndrome

The iliotibial band (ITB) – a sheet of connective tissue which runs down the outside of the thigh, from the hip to beyond the side of the knee – can rub against the femur above the knee. ITB syndrome is sometimes accompanied by 'snapping hip' which is the ITB brushing over the bursa sac, which rubs over the hip bone.

Symptoms: Pain along the outside of the knee or hip, especially when you stride.

Causes: If the iliotibial band is tight or the foot is forced inwards (as the lower foot is when you run on a camber), this bowing may cause friction between band and femur.

Treatment: Rest and ice will reduce acute inflammation, and changing sides of the road may help! Padding the outer side of the foot reduces the bow-leg effect, but you may need a full biomechanical assessment and possibly orthotics.

Prevention: Try to run on soft surfaces and avoid cambers, though this cannot fully compensate in the runner who is bow-legged to start with! Stretch several times a day, first the hamstrings, then the quads, then the ITB. The following are two good stretches for the ITB: if the inflammation is on your right side, stand with leg crossed behind the left and extend your left arm against something stable, like a wall, for support. Lean against the wall while you push your right hip out to the side. Keep your right foot anchored. You should feel the stretch in your right hip and down the outside of your right leg. Hold the position until the muscle relaxes. Release for a few seconds, then repeat. Do six to eight on that side, then an equal number on the opposite side, to keep things biomechanically 'even'.

Alternatively, lie on your back and pull your right knee towards your left shoulder. With your right hand on your knee, grab the right foot with your left hand and pull the knee closer to your shoulder with both hands. You should feel the stretch along the side of your leg. Hold until the muscle relaxes, release for a few seconds then repeat. Stretch both sides.

Osgood-Schlatter's disease
This condition usually affects growing boys between the ages of 10 and 14.
Symptoms: Pain at the front of and immediately below the knee, where the insertion of the patellar tendon becomes acutely inflamed.
Causes: Over-exercising, frequently accompanied by a growth spurt.
Treatment: Rest, ice packs and anti-inflammatories will reduce the pain, but as no damage normally occurs as a result of Osgood-Schlatter's Disease, you can continue to run providing you can take the pain. Avoid injections if possible, as the disease is self-limiting.
Prevention: Osgood-Schlatter's Disease is less likely in the child who plays a variety of sports, rather than concentrating on an individual one.

Synovitis
An inflammation of the synovium that lines the knee joint. If the tissues that line the knee joint become inflamed, they secrete an excess of lubricating fluid.

Basic treatments

How to use anti-inflammatories
Inflammation, common in running injuries, is characterised by pain and swelling, redness and warmth and can be treated with anti-inflammatory medications. Ibuprofen and naproxen sodium work well, as does aspirin. Follow the instructions on the bottle and take the medicines for one or two weeks. Always take them with food. Paracetamol is not an anti-inflammatory.

Some are available over the counter, some only on prescription. An acute injury usually requires a short course of a high-dose anti-inflammatory (NSAID), but many have side-effects and can cause stomach irritation or bleeding, dizziness, nausea, tinnitus (ringing in the ears) and asthma or hyperventilation. Consult a doctor before taking NSAIDs.

Symptoms: The swelling will cause discomfort and limit flexion, and sometimes extension and weight-bearing as well.
Causes: Although overuse may be involved, synovitis may be part of a generalised disease process which should be investigated.
Treatment: RICE and anti-inflammatories in the early stages. If the condition persists consult a doctor.
Prevention: Strengthening the quadriceps and building up your training gently should help in those cases where overuse is the cause.

Upper leg injuries

Hamstring pull
The hamstring muscles cover two joints, the hip and the knee. They can be strained throughout their length.
Symptoms: There is usually some severe

pain at the time of injury, followed by muscle spasm, loss of strength, and pain when you put weight on the legs.

Causes: Sudden contraction of the hamstrings, as when sprinting, is the most common cause. A pull may also be the result of overuse on a long run involving hill climbing, or may be caused by a runner having particularly strong quadriceps muscles compared to the hamstrings.

Treatment: RICE until full rehabilitation has occurred. Owing to the type of muscle within the hamstring, a pull can be slow to heal, and must be gently stretched and worked up to training. Severe tears will require the use of crutches.

Prevention: Runners often stretch the hamstrings wrongly – try to stretch them over one joint at a time. Don't forget to warm up!

Quadriceps strain

Long-distance runners occasionally tear the large muscles at the front of the thigh.

Symptoms: There will be a sudden pain, most probably when running downhill, and it is possible for the muscle to rupture completely. There is local tenderness and swelling.

Causes: Apart from running downhill, a sprint start when you're unprepared for it can cause a quadriceps strain.

Treatment: RICE until the muscle is fully stretched and rehabilitated.

Prevention: Proper stretching and warming up – inflexible quadriceps are more likely to tear.

Hip and groin injuries

Bursitis

Bursitis of the hip involves inflammation of the bursae that surround either of the bony swellings which are part of the hip joint. Bursae, fluid-filled sacs on the joint, can also affect the joints of the lower leg.

Symptoms: There is likely to be pain and tenderness, though often without much visible injury. There is usually a mild discomfort when you're at rest, and in more extreme cases this becomes severe pain when you're running. The range of movement of the hip is likely to be limited.

Causes: Once again, the finger points to overuse, though this may be compounded by direct bruising or a disease such as infection or arthritis.

Treatment: Although RICE may help, more chronic injuries will need full medical assessment, anti-inflammatory medication, and possibly a cortisone injection.

Prevention: A proper warm-up and stretching routine will help to limit the straining which frequently causes bursitis.

Strain

This vague term may imply injury to muscles, ligaments and tendons around the hip joint at the upper end of the femur (thigh bone).

Symptoms: There is usually pain when you make a particular movement, though there may also be tenderness or pressure, and even muscle spasm.

Causes: Overuse of the hip joint, though failure to stretch it through its complete range of movement will increase the likelihood of injury.

Treatment: RICE and ice massage will help, and physiotherapy, stretching and heat should be used to aid recovery in the later stages.

Prevention: Stretching and sensible training.

Groin strain

This is a non-specific title covering many injuries within the groin area. These include a hernia, osteitis pubis (inflammation of the junction of the pubic bones), a tear of the adductor muscles (which pull the thighs together), and injury to the muscles at the front of the hip.

Symptoms: Pain on moving the hip may be felt in both the groin and the abdomen or thigh. This is known as referred pain.

Causes: An inadequately trained hip which lacks a full range of movement is often to blame, though hernias appear to strike at will.

Treatment: If RICE, stretching and physiotherapy fail to produce early relief, medical assessment is vital. Chronic injuries take longer to heal, and if surgery is needed for a hernia, this shouldn't be delayed.

Prevention: As with all injuries in this area, a good range of movement will limit the likelihood of injury.

Lower back injuries

Lower back pain

Symptoms: Pain in the small of the back and sacroiliac joints where the spine joins the pelvis.

Causes: Running can be both a cause of lower back pain and a cure for it. It can help suppleness, but also increase tension in the over-trained. The pain is more likely in individuals with weak abdominal muscles.

Treatment: Sitting can actually put more strain on the back than running. If running isn't comfortable, swim, cycle or try some other activity. Walking is excellent.

In general lower back pain deserves full medical assessment – self-help may actually worsen the condition.

Prevention: This will depend on the cause, although a programme of stomach strengthening will help, as will regular stretching and strengthening exercises.

Try back extensions, lower-back stretches, pelvic tilts, bent-leg crunches and trunk twists.

Sciatica

The pain which can extend beyond the lower back, even to the ends of the toes, when a nerve emanating from the spine suffers pressure at some part of its length.

Symptoms: Initially you may simply feel a dull ache, but often there may be pain extending down one leg, which can cause weakness, numbness and a limp.

Causes: Congenital abnormalities of the lumbar and sacral vertebrae may combine with the jarring from running, together with biomechanical problems of the feet, knees or leg length, and cause poor posture which irritates or damages the sciatic nerve.

Treatment: Rest – many cases of sciatica get better in spite of medical treatment. When in severe pain, lie on the floor on your back with your hips and knees at right angles and your calves supported on a chair or stool.

Prevention: This may be impossible, but a supple lumbar spine and strong abdominal muscles will limit the chance of sciatica occurring.

Basic treatments

Stretching

When stretching make sure you feel the tension on the muscle you are stretching, which isn't necessarily the site of the injury. Do *not* bounce. Hold the stretch until you feel the muscles relax, usually between 15 and 30 seconds.

It's best to stretch warm muscles, but it's OK to stretch gently when you haven't warmed up. Where stretching is indicated as part of a treatment for an injury, it's best to stretch several times a day.

Abdominal injuries

Stitch

Symptoms: A sharp pain or spasm in the lower abdomen which occurs while you are running.

Causes: A spasm of the diaphragm (the large, dome-shaped muscle dividing the abdomen from the chest).

Treatment: It may help while running to take a deep breath and hold it, thus stretching the diaphragm.

Prevention: An irritated diaphragm is more likely to go into spasm, so you should eat your pre-race meal at least three hours before competing. Drinking plenty of fluid helps to keep the intestinal organs supple and pliable. A stitch is a symptom of lack of training, for the diaphragm has to be trained in the same way as other muscles.

Muscle injuries

Bruise (or contusion)

Symptoms: A bruise will almost certainly result in local muscle spasm as a result of bleeding at the site of injury.

Causes: This injury is usually the result of a direct blow, which causes small blood vessels to rupture or burst. The escape of blood into the muscle tissue causes additional irritation, with local pain and spasm.

Treatment: Use RICE initially and repeat for at least 48 hours, and even longer if the condition continues. Attempting to run it off may simply worsen it and prolong the time you lose to running. During rehabilitation, walk before you run.

Cramps

A sustained but involuntary contraction of muscles.

Symptoms: The most noticeable is

always pain, though if you touch it the muscle will feel very hard and sore.

Causes: There is no single cause of cramp, but contributory factors can include the worsening of a slight muscle strain, running without warming up, dehydration, fatigue and an electrolyte imbalance.

Treatment: Gently stretch and massage the muscle after the initial spasm relaxes. Heat and physiotherapy may relieve the pain.

Prevention: Ensure that you're well hydrated and have a balanced diet containing electrolytes, especially in warm and humid climates.

Rupture

A complete rupture of a muscle can occur following a major sprain. The muscles at the front and back of the thighs and calves can all be affected.

Symptoms: There may be acute immediate pain with a visible bulge, though in some cases shock (from the bleeding) may be more noticeable than pain. Any attempt to contract the muscle will fail to move the joint.

Causes: Ruptures are not very common. they are most likely to occur in muscles which are already damaged or within tendons.

Treatment: Surgical reconstruction may not be required, as other muscles may develop to perform the task of the injured one. A full medical assessment is vital.

Spasm

A form of cramp, but often more sustained.

Symptoms: A spasm will cause severe local pain and tenderness which will stop you running.

Causes: As with cramps, dehydration, a previous injury or lack of a warm-up may all contribute to a spasm.

Treatment: Stop running and try to

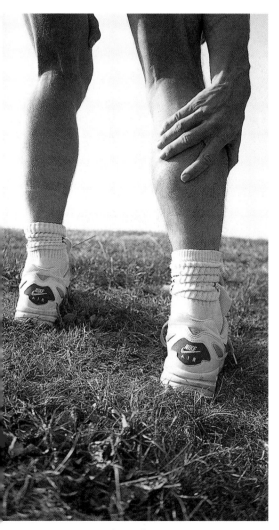

*Warming up and stretching
reduces the risk of strains.*

stretch the muscle gently. If it relaxes quickly, it's probably all right to run on. If the spasm returns, stop and treat it as you would a strain.
Prevention: As with cramps.

Strain

Although it may also be referred to as a pull, a strain usually involves some tearing within the muscle or tendon structure.

Symptoms: Although overuse strains may not produce discomfort until several hours after exercise, they may also occur suddenly as a result of over-stretching, in which case you'll be forced to pull up lame. Spasm and swelling from torn blood vessels may also occur.
Causes: A strain can result from overuse or over-training and over-racing.
Treatment: Use RICE and rest until the bleeding is contained and comfortable. This will probably take 48 hours. Resume training by walking slowly. You will probably need a rest period of several days before you can run.
Prevention: Proper warming up and stretching will help to reduce the likelihood of injury, as will a sensible, gradual approach to speedwork.

General problems and disorders

Anaemia

Any reduction in either the number or volume of red blood cells can produce this condition.
Causes: Iron deficiency caused by blood loss covers only a minority of cases of anaemia. If you are anaemic, you may be suffering from a vitamin or nutritional deficiency, or a disease of almost any organ within the body. In short, anaemia needs medical investigation.
Prevention: A well-balanced diet will only prevent certain forms of anaemia.

Anorexia nervosa and bulimia

These are both psychiatric conditions: anorexia is self-starvation and an intense fear of becoming fat, while bulimia is usually characterised by binge eating and self-induced vomiting. Both disorders are more common in women. The medical implications include the possibility of starvation, dehydration and brittle bones.

Both these illnesses require psychiatric and medical help.

Arrhythmia

Arrhythmia, i.e. an irregular heartbeat, is a common complaint, even among healthy individuals. While it may be a symptom of disease, it appears to be more common in fit athletes with slow pulse rates.

Symptoms: A slight shudder over the chest in minor cases, extending to dizziness, blackouts and chest pain in more severe ones, indicates a condition which requires urgent medical investigation.

Causes: Some runners who ingest large quantities of caffeine in tea, coffee or cola may benefit from reducing their caffeine intake. Two other common causes are an overactive thyroid gland and alcohol abuse.

Athlete's foot

A contagious fungal infection of the foot.

Symptoms: Initially there may be a few spots and redness, particularly between the third and fourth toes, but these may spread, and you may experience burning, itching and loss of skin.

Treatment: Anti-fungal creams and powders will cure most infections, but won't work if the feet aren't clean and dry. Use the products two or three times a day for two to four weeks, and continue to use them for one to two weeks after symptoms are gone. The fungus remains even after the irritation disappears. To relieve itching, soak your feet in baking soda mixed with water. Remove dead skin with a pumice stone, or rub fine sandpaper along the bottoms of your feet and discard the sandpaper. Frequent changes of socks and shoes are essential.

Prevention: Athlete's foot fungus is ubiquitous and thrives in dark, moist places. Clean, dry socks will limit its opportunity to colonise.

Chronic fatigue syndrome

A recently described phenomenon, also know as ME (Myalgic Encephalomyelitis) and yuppie 'flu, among other things.

Symptoms: Usually, some form of infection – probably a virus which causes a sore throat, lymph-node swelling, muscle weakness and headaches – fails to resolve itself, leaving the sufferer with debilitating fatigue whenever they undertake any exertion. It sometimes occurs in epidemics. Although viral studies will sometimes indicate a cause, they prove negative more often than not. Many sufferers become clinically depressed.

Treatment: Running must be drastically reduced. While there is no set pattern of treatment which is uniformly successful, gentle exercise to sub-exhaustion levels, combined with treatment of the clinical depression, appears to offer the best compromise. However, many sufferers experience setbacks before a full recovery is achieved. Good-quality sleep is also important.

Dehydration

Running in any weather can cause excessive sweat loss, though this is more likely in hot weather, and the resulting loss of body fluids and minerals causes dehydration. As little as 2 per cent dehydration will have a negative effect on your running performance.

Symptoms: A dry mouth and thirst in the early stages may be followed by dark-coloured urine (and, eventually no urination at all), low blood pressure, dry skin and confusion. Dehydration can be fatal.

Treatment: Stop running, go to a cool place and drink plenty of fluids. If the condition is severe, this will probably have to be given intravenously.

Prevention: Everyone's fluid needs vary. You know you're getting enough if you void large volumes of clear urine at least six times a day.

To determine how much liquid to take during a run or race, you need to know your sweat rate, and that can vary from 2 and 8 pints an hour. Weigh yourself nude before a timed training run and then again after. One pound of weight loss equals one pint of water loss. Calculate your sweat rate and use this to determine your fluid needs during a run or a race. Diarrhoea can cause severe dehydration and should be treated with electrolyte-replacement drinks.

Exercise-induced asthma

This condition appears to be on the increase, though that may simply be because it is better diagnosed nowadays. The sufferer will probably complain of chest tightness, shortness of breath, wheezing and coughing after even minimal effort. This may be related to a family history of allergy.

Treatment: Exercise-induced asthma is reversible with rest, but most sufferers require treatment using inhaled bronchodilators, or even steroids. Children may find a substance called sodium cromoglycate more effective. These drugs are banned in tablet or liquid form by the International Olympic Committee and can only be taken through inhalation.

Prevention: Before a run or race, warm up for about 10 minutes. Then start running hard, which may cause the asthmatic response, triggering the release of adrenaline, which then dilates the bronchial tubes. Run hard for five minutes then slow for five minutes, repeat several times, then walk. Stretch and walk a little more. Perform this routine 15 to 30 minutes before you race or run. The intensity of this warm-up results in a refractory period of between 60 to 90 minutes during which you should be able to exercise without an asthma attack.

Cold and dry conditions or mouth-breathing may worsen the condition, so sufferers may benefit from wearing a mask. Many Olympic champions have been asthmatics, but have learnt how to treat the condition by using suitable medication.

Anxiety can exacerbate an asthma attack. Some experts recommend 30-minute relaxation sessions several times a week to teach you to relax readily at times of stress.

Exertional headache

This tends to occur immediately after a run and may cause nausea and vomiting as well as pain. Treated like a migraine, i.e. with aspirin or paracetamol, it will usually subside rapidly. Exertional headaches are especially likely to afflict those running at altitude or who are dehydrated.

Flat feet

A flat foot is one in which the longitudinal arch drops towards the ground. In runners this leads to over-pronation, which alters the movement of the bones within the feet and contributes to foot and leg injuries.

Symptoms: You may experience pain under the arch and/or on the opposite outer side of the ankle during running, which can worsen the condition.

Causes: Flat feet are frequently inherited, but may be worsened by poor footwear and training.

Treatment: After a time, most runners with flat feet will experience pain. Orthotics and anti-pronation shoes are undoubtedly the best treatment, and physiotherapy can strengthen the small muscles of the feet.

Gastrointestinal problems

For runners, gastrointestinal problems usually mean 'runner's trots', or diarrhoea. Other sometimes related symptoms commonly include cramps, gas and heartburn. Runner's trots occur in as many as one-third of all runners and may be even more common among women. Running has been scientifically proven to hasten the passage of food through the bowel. In certain circumstances this can lead to diarrhoea and loss of vital fluids.

Prevention: Regular patterns of training and eating will usually allow the body to get into the habit of emptying the bowel before running. Excessive intake of dietary fibre and many sugary products can contribute to the problem: over time, runners will find out what they can and cannot eat.

Haematuria

The technical term for blood in the urine.

Symptoms: Microscopic amounts of blood within the urine aren't visible to the naked eye, while some redness may be due to causes other than blood (such as eating beetroot!). Where blood cells are 'mashed' by running on hard surfaces, the resulting condition is called haemoglobinuria.

Treatment: Blood in the urine must always be investigated. It may well be a benign symptom, but it could also indicate a more serious disease.

Prevention: Haemoglobinuria is less common in those who run with some urine in the bladder, and who drink often during a long race.

Heat illness

This category includes heat exhaustion and heat-stroke, together with other illnesses caused by prolonged exposure to heat and high humidity, which causes the body core temperature to rise and produces dehydration and a failure of the body's cooling system.

Symptoms: The skin may be perversely cool or moist and pale, but the runner appears confused. In heat-stroke, the skin becomes hot and dry. These conditions are serious, and the runner may well have to be hospitalised.

Treatment: Drink fluids, cease exercise and get into the shade. Seek medical advice. If at all serious, start intravenous fluids.

Hypothermia

Because of prolonged exposure to cold conditions, the body's core temperature is lowered.

Symptoms: You may find yourself shivering, feeling cold, and unable to perform even simple tasks without apparent mental difficulties.

Treatment: A hypothermic runner should be re-warmed with hot drinks and wrapped up well in space blankets and other warm clothing. Do not use hot-water bottles.

Prevention: Run well covered in several layers of clothing (the air gaps in between help to retain heat), and avoid getting wet. If running in cold weather, try to run into the wind at the start, so that you can return to base with it behind you.

Jockstrap rash

A skin infection of the groin area, caused by a fungus.

Symptoms: Red, itchy patches of skin in the groin, thigh and buttock area, which can become painful. The skin may be secondarily infected by bacteria.

Causes: Jockstrap rash is more likely in hot and humid weather, when you sweat excessively and the resulting friction can damage the skin.

Treatment: An anti-fungal cream or ointment will usually destroy the germ, but it is less likely to colonise in the first place if the skin is clean and dry.

Prevention: Loose-fitting underwear that is clean and dry limits the opportunities for the fungus to colonise the skin.

Leg-length discrepancy

No human beings are symmetrical, and many have legs of different lengths. This may not affect most people, but any difference greater than half an inch can cause problems for the runner.

You can test yourself at home to determine the extent of any leg-length discrepancy. In your underwear, stand in front of a mirror. Look to see if your shoulders are level (if you've played a lot of throwing sports, your dominant shoulder will hang lower and can confuse the issue). Look at your pelvis, then let your body sag and look again. Put your fingers on the body areas in front of your hip and look to see if they are level. If they are not, place magazines under the foot of the shorter leg to determine the extent of the discrepancy.

Symptoms: Runners tend to compensate for leg-length discrepancy, but they may develop pain in the knees, hip, groin or lower back. The pelvis has to tilt to compensate for the discrepancy, and the spine may be affected. The only way to obtain an accurate diagnosis is by measuring the bones on an X-ray film.

Treatment: Orthotics or built-up shoes can cure the condition, though many runners simply compensate by using the road camber to their advantage. Suitable physiotherapy can cure many more specific symptoms.

Menstrual dysfunction

Many female runners suffer from some form of problem with their periods. Those who are very thin and run high mileages may suffer from amenorrhoea (the absence of periods), while dysmenorrhoea (painful periods) or menorrhagia (very heavy periods) may make you feel tired and anaemic.

Treatment: There are now many methods of curing difficult periods (both hormonal and non-hormonal), and no woman should hesitate to seek the advice of her GP or a gynaecologist if she is concerned.

Osteoporosis

This condition, which more commonly affects women, involves a loss of bone density. This occurs naturally later in life, particularly after the menopause, but is less likely in those women who have normal periods and take regular exercise.

Prevention: Running is a particularly good method of preventing osteoporosis, as it is a weight-bearing activity. The maintenance of normal oestrogen levels (which does not occur in women with amenorrhoea), and a diet including reasonable quantities of calcium, will limit the tendency to osteoporosis and bone fractures.

Over-training syndrome

The result of running too far and/or too often, something which is frequently not recognised by runners.

Symptoms: Minor aches and pains which persist, or general over-tiredness. Your morning pulse rate may be raised, or you may become more prone to minor infections. You will never feel fresh during training.

Treatment: Proper coaching, with a rest built in. Some runners would definitely benefit from a month's complete rest from running: persuading them to do so is another matter.

Prevention: It is particularly important to recover from marathons and other long-distance races before training for another event.

Runner's nipple

Causes: The nipples may become chafed by a tight or coarse fabric vest, and this is worsened if dirt or wetness increases the friction.

Prevention: Apply a plaster or some petroleum jelly before you run.

Facts about running injuries

1. Women are more prone to injury than men. As they have wider hips than men they tend to overpronate more, which can lead to a range of problems. Women also have more elastic tissue which makes them more liable to joint and ligament damage.
2. About 20 per cent of runners seek medical care for their running-related aches and pains during a typical year.
3. There is little connection between body weight and risk of injury.
4. About 75 per cent of runners who seek medical attention report that their recovery is 'good' or 'excellent', and 65 per cent of runners report that they are running pain-free after eight weeks of treatment. Iliotibial band syndrome appears to require the longest recovery period.
5. The part of your body most at risk depends on your preferred race distance. Marathon runners suffer mainly foot problems, middle-distance runners have more back and hip troubles, while sprinters tend to suffer more hamstring and muscle tears.
6. Compared to marathon runners, sprinters have about double the injury rate per hour of actual training.
7. Spring and summer are high season for injuries.
8. The best direct injury predictor may be the number of miles you ran last month.
9. Some studies suggest that aggressive, tense and compulsive runners have higher risks of injury than their more relaxed peers. These personalities also have more multiple injuries and lose twice as much training time when an injury actually occurs.
10. If you were injured last year, your chance of injuring yourself again this year is increased by 50 per cent.

Source: *Runner's World* research.

Injury treatments

With the wide array of potential injuries likely to afflict a runner, it is hardly surprising that the means of treating those injuries has become equally vast. Traditionally the first call, for anything other than a minor problem, has always been the local GP. While that should still be the case for those seeking a precise diagnosis of the problem, there are a number of options both in mainstream medicine and the alternative branch of the profession for those seeking an active treatment of an injury. The following is an explanation of the various treatment options available and the benefits to particular types of injuries.

Acupuncture

An ancient art based on the theory that the body is full of energy pathways, and that there is an ideal state of optimum energy flow. This therapy involves treatment at 'trigger points' which relieves areas of stress to restore normal energy flow – and thus, optimum comfort and performance. While acupressure is non-invasive, using pressure applied with fingers, thumbs and the heel of the hand, acupuncture involves the insertion of fine, sterile needles to a depth of a few millimetres. Its advocates claim that acupuncture is especially effective in reviving exhausted and overstressed muscles.

Applied kinesiology

A fairly new spin-off from chiropractics. The applied kinesiologist studies movement to identify areas of muscular weakness, and then prescribes strengthening exercises to help stave off injuries that may be 'waiting to happen'. In treatment, the applied kinesiologist relies heavily on standard chiropractic techniques, and may even borrow from traditional physical therapy techniques and acupuncture theory.

Aqua running

Running in water. A fairly new alternative for injured runners, aqua running allows them to keep 'running' while avoiding the normal stress of impact. It also offers the extra benefit of resistance. If you try to move with the same speed as you would on land, you will meet 850 times the resistance! Wear a flotation device or just run in the swimming pool. Devote the same time to warming up, cooling down and stretching that you would on dry land.

Arthroscopy

A diagnostic or surgical procedure in which the surgeon examines the inside of a joint. It is less invasive than traditional surgery, requiring just one or two tiny holes in the joint, into which the surgeon inserts the arthroscope – an instrument with a system of lights and lenses which allows them to view the inside of a joint. Commonly used on the knee or ankle joint, arthroscopy requires considerably less time for rehabilitation than traditional surgery. Patients are usually walking within two days and running in a week or two.

Chiropractic

Manual manipulation of the spine to achieve a proper skeletal orientation with regard to the other systems of the body, especially the neural and muscular systems. By relieving pressure on the nerves and correcting these relationships, chiropractic realignment can relieve discomfort and enhance performance.

Electrical muscle stimulation (EMS)

Otherwise known as electrostimulation or electrotherapy, a treatment and preventive for muscular atrophy which comes with immobilisation of a limb. It also may be helpful in reducing swelling and pain around an injured joint, and for treating spasms.

Heat therapy

Treatment involving hot compresses, whirlpools, ultrasound, heat lamps or hot pads. It is generally used after ice therapy has helped to seal and stop fluid accumulation at the point of injury. Heat promotes healing by dilating the small blood vessels in the area, increasing blood flow and the influx of healing nutrients. It also helps to reduce the pain and spasm sometimes associated with muscle injury.

Hydrotherapy

Water-related treatment which includes everything from swimming to underwater therapy. Some devices (whirlpools) mimic a massage effect, others make use of hot or cold water. With acute injuries, hydrotherapy can be used to chill the area to prevent further tissue damage. With some injuries, heat helps to reduce soreness and restore mobility.

Laser therapy

Therapy involving the shooting of a helium-neon laser into the injured tissue to increase circulation, thus speeding the arrival of healing nutrients and the removal of wastes and by-products.

Massage

Therapy ranging from the gentle, soothing strokes of Swedish massage to the deep, cross-friction strokes of the Cyriax method. Shiatsu massage, or acupressure, uses pressure on specific trigger points to relieve areas of biomechanical stress. All forms of massage can speed athletic recovery by soothing tense muscles and speeding the flow of healing nutrients (through the bloodstream) to the injured areas; the latter also helps to flush lactic acid and other metabolic waste products out of the system. The Cyriax method works deep into the muscles to break up scar tissue and adhesions. Massage also has psychological benefits.

Microcurrent therapy

A technique which uses a low-level current of electricity to restore electrical balance to injured tissue. It is based on the theory that since all tissues have electrical charges, there is an optimum electrical balance which is disturbed by injury. Microcurrent therapy is an acupuncture-type stimulation achieved using electricity instead of needles.

Orthotics

Devices which are custom-made by a podiatrist or orthopaedic surgeon and inserted into shoes to protect and support the foot, and to correct musculoskeletal misalignment (caused for example, by flat feet or leg-length discrepancy). Over-the-counter 'foot supports', in contrast, are not necessarily corrective, although their added cushioning and support may be beneficial.

Osteopathy

The first complementary medical treatment to enter the mainstream. This form of treatment is extremely popular with elite and non-elite runners, both as a long-term preventative maintenance programme and to treat actual injuries. It's a system of healing that works on the physical structure of the body using joint and muscle manipulation, massage and stretching techniques.

Pneumatic braces

Air-filled braces which were used initially in the treatment of leg stress fractures, but are now being used for sprains as well. With these braces, it is possible for the athlete to continue training runs while healing; the brace allows flexion and extension of the foot, while prohibiting the lateral movement.

Rehabilitative exercise bike

An isokinetic machine used for rehabilitation. It offers 'accommodating resistance' – you set the speed of the bike, and it provides resistance which relates directly to the energy you invest. You can find these machines at many sports-medicine clinics and fitness centres.

Transcutaneous electrical nerve stimulation (TENS)

In this treatment, a device sends electrical signals to nerves near an injury site; the constant neural stimulation masks or blocks pain signals so that an athlete can go on with rehabilitation exercise. TENS usually consists of two small electrodes connected to a hand-sized dual channel stimulator; the athlete can adjust the amplitude, gradually increasing it to a comfortable intensity. TENS reportedly reduces muscle atrophy, joint stiffness and the need for narcotic pain relievers.

Ultrasound

Use of high-frequency sound waves outside the normal range of human hearing to produce deep heat which is applied directly to an injured area. Ultrasound sends heat deeper into the tissues than any other treatment. This decades-old procedure, which is given in a series of six- to ten-minute treatments, is among the most commonly prescribed healing strategies. It is painless and accurate.

Preventative measures

The best advice anyone can give you about injuries, is not to get injured at all. While that may be a near impossible task for many runners, you can certainly cut down on the number of injuries you sustain by following some sensible preventative measures.

This is not just a matter of warming up, stretching and cooling down properly, which will certainly help to cut down on the number of muscular problems, it has as much to do with your attitude to running.

Be realistic about the goals you set yourself; that is not to say you shouldn't aspire to improve, merely that you have to realise that you may never run a sub-four-minute mile. Similarly, try to get away from a belief that miles and speed are everything in a training programme. Harder and further are not necessarily better. A lot of people have a tendency to overstrain, believing that high mileage is the only route to every goal.

It may be a good idea at this point to following that age-old maxim, a change is as good as a rest. You can relieve much of the strain of a rigorous training programme by mixing in regular cycling, swimming or walking routines. These will complement rather than detract from your running, keep your legs fresh and reduce the burn-out or staleness that result from heavy mileage.

Coming back from injury

Returning from running injury requires the same kind of dedication as the sport itself. According to recent studies high levels of self-motivation are critical to the rehabilitation process, although you do have to be careful. With runners in particular, a high degree of motivation can become a problem by denying that the injury even exists. Psychologists say that successful injury recovery requires an element of acceptance that frequently runs counter to a runner's sense of economy and drive to succeed. Runners, in particular, have to realise that what they may see as laziness when they take time off is, in fact, the greatest possible act of diligence. Here are a few tips to speed up the recovery:

1. **Get good medical advice.**
   It's a lot easier to complete a rehabilitation programme when you feel confident about the advice given. If obtaining the best possible medical advice means obtaining more than one opinion, then that's what you should do.

2. **Try not to be emotional about the injury.**
   Becoming depressed or angry about having to take an injury break from running can actually cause the release of stress hormones that may impede healing. The more you relax and accept your injuries the quicker they heal.

3. **Look at your injury as an opportunity.**
   Use your recovery time to pursue other interests or to spend more time with family and friends. Don't stop those pursuits when you're back on your feet.

4. **Don't worry about leaning on others.**
   Talking with others – especially those who have been through similar experiences – can give you confidence that your down time can propel you to better performances than before.

A good way of controlling your training programme and tailoring it to your individual needs is with a heart-rate monitor, which will tell you when it's time to cut back and when you are over-doing things. Even without a heart-rate monitor your body will warn you if you start to push too hard.

Everyone has a maximum training threshold and if you start to find that you have symptoms that are getting progressively worse each time you go out then it's time to back off.

You don't have to be obsessional about it, but you should be aware of symptoms within yourself that suggest you are overdoing things. Learn to recognise the difference between fatigue and exhaustion. You should be tired at the end of a run, but you shouldn't always be exhausted. Fatigue which becomes continuous and which you find difficult to recover from is a sure sign of exhaustion.

Don't ignore lower-limb pain. This is the body's natural warning system. With experience, you should be able to distinguish between good and bad pain. But an injury or niggle left untreated is likely to develop into something much worse. Although there are very few injuries that you can't continue running with, avoid the urge to run through a problem. Few injuries will improve without treatment or rest and most will eventually degenerate into something more serious.

Running shoes and injuries

Your running shoes are confusingly both one of the most common causes of injury and also one of the best ways of preventing them. The key is to find a pair which match your foot type, your running style, your running habits and

Carefully chosen shoes will help to keep you off the sidelines.

injury history (see Chapter 4 on equipment for more details). As a general rule wear shoes which are big enough! When you run, your feet elongate and your toes spread. If your shoes aren't long enough, your toes will become sore from the constant pressure and irritation. Eventually, this can cause blisters and 'runner's toe'. The space between your longest toe and the end of the shoe should measure about the width of your thumbnail.

Heavier runners should stay away from super-lightweight shoes. Don't sacrifice protection for the sake of a small saving in shoe weight: you'll probably pay the price later with plantar fasciitis, forefoot bruises, Achilles tendinitis or knee problems.

They should also look for shoes with midsoles made of polyurethane, or a combination of polyurethane and EVA (ethylene vinyl acetate, a light foam which is now commonly moulded into midsoles). These are preferable to conventional 100 per cent EVA midsoles; polyurethane offers more density and firmness, which is especially important for tall and heavy runners. Also, look for solid rubber outsoles.

Keep track of your mileage and plan to replace your shoes every 400–500 miles. By then, the support and cushioning structures of the shoes are breaking down, hindering their ability to protect you from the stresses of running.

Here are some shoe-buying guidelines for those who are prone to the four most common running injuries:

1. Runners with knee problems commonly overpronate. Select shoes with excellent motion control and

The complete cool-down

A majority of runners do not warm up or stretch properly. Fewer still cool down after a training session. They are making a mistake. The cool-down is the best way to recover while preparing your body and mind for the next workout, which is always the most important. Here's how to do it.

1. Finish every session with 10–12 minutes of easy jogging. This will decrease the stress on your cardiovascular system, ease your leg muscles and relax your body and mind.
2. Stretch. In most cases stretching after a training session is far more beneficial for muscle flexibility than doing it before you run. In fact, the latest research suggests runners who stretch before they run have more injuries than those who do it afterwards.
3. Ice painful muscles for 10 minutes at a time. Run ice on the areas where you feel pain for a mere 10 minutes rather than the complete RICE workout for a more severe injury. Stop icing for 10 minutes then repeat the dose.
4. Eat carbohydrate and protein. Runners who eat 100 calories of carbohydrate every 15 minutes for a couple of hours after exercising will greatly increase their muscle glycogen stores, according to recent research. Other studies claim that eating 60 calories of protein (such as in a tub of yoghurt) will also help replenish glycogen stores and repair muscle damage.
5. Try to relax your mind and think positively about the session. The first point will help your body to recover, but it's equally important that you leave your session mentally refreshed. If you are mentally pleased with a workout you'll be ready to tackle the next one with freshness and enthusiasm.

stability features, plus firm – but not stiff – midsole cushioning.

2. Another problem associated with overpronating: Shinsplints hobble more novice runners than any other injury, because these runners' shin muscles are unaccustomed to the excessive motion. Again, the best choice is a shoe with good motion-control features, particularly those which enhance rearfoot stability. Another beneficial feature is a firm, multi-density midsole especially configured to help absorb and disperse shock.

3. Also linked to overpronating, Achilles tendinitis responds well to shoes with good motion-control and stability.

4. As heel spurs are often aggravated by external pressure, your shoes should offer good rearfoot shock absorption. Also, because heel spurs are often associated with chronic plantar fasciitis, look to protect the plantar fascia with motion-control features and shoe stiffness. Choosing the best stiffness is a bit tricky, because, while stiffness inhibits the foot from twisting (and thus irritating the plantar fascia), too stiff a shoe will irritate the plantar fascia through impact. A good compromise is a combination-lasted shoe, i.e. one with a fibre-board last in the rearfoot for stability, and stitching only in the forefoot for flexibility and comfort.

Organisations

For more information on injury prevention and treatment, contact:

British Association of Sports and Medicine
St Bartholomew's Medical College, Charterhouse Square, London EC1M 6BQ; 0171 253 3244

British Chiropractic Association
29 Whitley Street, Reading, Berks RG2 0EG; 01734 757557

British Homeopathic Association
27a Devonshire Street, London W1N 1RJ; 0171 935 2163

British Olympic Medical Centre
Northwick Park Hospital, Watford Road, Harrow, Middx HA1 3UJ; 0181 864 3232

Chartered Society of Physiotherapists
14 Bedford Row, London WC1R 4ED: 0171 242 1941

General Council and Register of Osteopaths
56 London Street, Reading, Berks RG1 4SQ; 01734 576585

London College of Massage
5–6 Newman Passage, London W1P 3PF; 0171 323 3574

National Sports Medicine Institute
St Bartholomew's Medical College, Charterhouse Square, London EC1M 6BQ; 0171 253 3244

Society of Chiropodists
53 Welbeck Street, London SW1M 7HE; 0171 486 3381

15 Nutrition

To many people food is something which simply stops them feeling hungry. They eat what they want to whenever they need to satisfy their appetite. But for runners and anyone who takes part in sport, food is more important than that. It is the fuel that provides the energy to exercise and eating the right food is the key to lifelong health. No food will make you an instant champion and you will never eat your way to faster times, but good nutrition habits will help you to get the maximum enjoyment out of your running.

But most runners lead busy lives and juggling work commitments with a social life as well as a daily run barely leaves any time to think about healthy eating. They often put tremendous effort into choosing the right running shoes or the right clothing, but just grab the easiest and quickest, which is not always the healthiest, food to eat.

This chapter will help you to devise a personal eating plan to suit your own lifestyle but without spending too much time or money. By learning to eat the right food at the right time, you will be doing your body and your running a huge favour.

Where do you get the energy to run?

The answer is simple – from the food you eat. That is why no amount of extra training will substitute for a poor diet.

Dieticians and nutritionists describe any food or drink in terms of its nutrient content, that is the individual chemicals which make up food and which are vital to health. The best sports diet incorporates all the major nutrients – carbohydrates, fats, proteins, vitamins and minerals. You can only get the right balance of all these nutrients by eating a variety of wholesome foods.

Every food contains different amounts of different nutrients. Fresh, unprocessed food generally has a better nutrient content, but no food is actually bad for you. Even fish and chips can fit into a sports diet provided that they are eaten in moderation and provided you make a low fat choice for your other meals that day.

The government produces figures for the amount of each nutrient that is needed to keep the average body in a healthy state. These Recommended Daily Amounts (RDAs) are based on estimates for a healthy adult and are only a rough guide to healthy eating. In reality everyone has different nutritional requirements and, as a runner, it is quite likely that you might need a higher intake of some nutrients than a sedentary person.

The easiest way to make sure that you are getting all the nutrients your body requires is to choose a variety of foods from the following groups every day:

Fruit and vegetables
You can't beat fresh fruit and vegetables for nutrient-packed foods. Both are full of vitamins C and A as well as fibre, potassium and carbohydrates.

Fibre, vitamins, minerals and carbohydrates – vegetables have them all.

How much? As a guideline, you should be aiming to eat at least five portions of fruit and vegetables every day, more if you can. One portion is a medium green salad, one medium-sized piece of fruit, a medium serving of vegetables or a large glass of fresh fruit juice.

Good choices Vegetables tend to be more nutrient-dense than fruits and dark green or brightly coloured vegetables, like broccoli, green peppers, carrots and tomatoes, have the best nutritional value of all. Bananas are high in potassium and fibre as well as being easy to digest, which makes them one of the best sports fruits around, and freshly squeezed orange juice has more nutrients than most other fruit

juices. Dried fruit also makes a healthy snack as it is packed with carbohydrates and potassium.

Cereals and starchy foods
Along with fruit and vegetables, this group should form the backbone of a perfect sports diet. These carbohydrate-rich, high-fibre foods provide your muscles with the fuel they need to keep running and without them your body simply won't have enough energy to perform at its best.

How much? You should be aiming to eat between six and twelve portions per day – one portion is a small serving of pasta, a slice of bread or an average-sized bowl of breakfast cereal.

Good choices Unsweetened breakfast cereal, bread, starchy vegetables such as potatoes, pasta and rice. Bagels, rye crispbreads and rice cakes make perfect high-carbo, low-fat snacks to eat between meals and some breakfast cereals have the advantage of being fortified with vitamins and minerals.

Milk and dairy products
Dairy foods are also a key part of a sports diet because they contain protein and riboflavin, but most importantly because they are high in calcium, the nutrient which is needed to keep your bones strong and healthy. It is not only growing children and teenagers that need a calcium-rich diet; it is just as important for adults too. Bones need calcium until they stop growing when you reach around thirty years of age and, after that, as a normal part of ageing, they will slowly start to lose their density. A low bone density, or osteoporosis, leaves your bones much more susceptible to fractures, but it can be offset to some extent by a high-calcium diet combined with regular exercise.

How much? Women, who are more

prone to osteoporosis, and runners under twenty should aim for four servings of calcium-rich foods per day and adult men should aim for three. One serving is equivalent to a regular carton of yoghurt, three slices of cheese or a small glass of milk.

Good choices Milk, cheese and low-fat yoghurt. Tinned fish with bones (such as tuna and salmon) are rich sources of calcium as are some dark green vegetables such as broccoli.

Meat, fish and their protein relatives

Although the pre-event steak is no longer considered to be the ideal preparation for a race, some protein foods are essential in a good sports diet. Your body needs protein primarily to help build and maintain muscles and tendons but protein-rich foods also supply some B vitamins as well as iron and zinc. In spite of popular legend, extra protein doesn't turn into muscles and won't make you any stronger.

How much? About two portions every day. Animal proteins, such as meat and fish, contain the most essential amino acids, but a good mixture of vegetable proteins will also meet your requirements.

Good choices Lean cuts of meat, fish or poultry. Both meat-eaters and vegetarians should try to eat more vegetable proteins such as peas, nuts, lentils, seeds and tofu.

Are supplements the easy way to get all the nutrients you need?

Manufacturers certainly spend plenty of time and money trying to convince you that this is the case and that, as a runner, you need more vitamins and minerals than the average person. In fact, a balanced diet will provide you with all the nutrients that you need and supplements should only be taken to complement a healthy eating regime, not to replace it. It doesn't matter how much money you spend buying supplements, you still need to eat the right foods if the pills and potions are to have any benefit at all.

Because you run regularly, you naturally expend more energy than the average person. But the likelihood is that, like most runners, you also eat more than sedentary people which means that you automatically replace any nutrients that are lost. Only if you don't eat a balanced diet or if you consistently under-eat at meal times do you risk becoming deficient in any of the vitamins and minerals.

If you do have a deficiency, it will definitely affect your running performance and taking a supplement will correct the problem. But it is important to remember that consuming too much of some vitamins and minerals can actually be dangerous. It is very rare for anyone to overdose on vitamins from normal food, but too many supplements of the fat-soluble vitamins A,D,E and K, for instance, will be stored in the body and can be harmful.

In short, more is not better when it comes to vitamin and mineral supplements.

Is fluid as important as food?

Just as eating the right amount and combination of foods can enhance your running, drinking the right fluids at the right times can also help to keep your body in tip-top condition so that you can perform at your best.

Every time you run you lose some fluid, either through sweating or through the water vapour released as you breathe. In general, the amount of fluid that you lose will depend on how hard you are running and how long you are running for as well as on the weather – if it is hot and humid you will lose a lot more fluid

Stay hydrated – an average runner can lose two pints of fluid in an hour.

than if it is cold. Some people sweat more than others, but the average runner will lose around two pints of fluid for every hour that they are on their feet.

It is essential that you drink enough to replace these losses, since body fluids have important roles to play such as transporting glucose to your working muscles and eliminating waste products through urine and blood. Of course, fluid

replacement also means that your body can maintain a constant temperature through sweating which has the effect of dissipating heat through the skin.

If you don't drink enough before, during and after a race or training session you risk becoming dehydrated which will not only put paid to any hopes of a fast time, it can also result in serious medical complications.

A dehydrated runner will lose the ability to sweat efficiently, which causes the body temperature to rise so that they become more dehydrated and so on. If your body fluid drops by only 2 per cent during a race (that is less than 1.5kg for a 70kg person), then you might experience dizziness or feel light-headed and nauseous. A further drop of 4–5 per cent of your body weight would mean that you would probably only be able to run at around two-thirds of your normal potential. Eventually your body would become so fatigued that you simply wouldn't be able to run another step.

There is no way to stop your body from losing fluid when you run but you can easily prevent excessive fluid losses by adopting a good hydration programme. These are the golden rules for successful hydration:

1. Get into the habit of drinking fluids every time you eat.
2. Eat watery foods such as tomatoes, oranges, cucumber and other fruits or salad vegetables to enhance your fluid intake.
3. Avoid drinking caffeine-based fluids such as coffee, tea or cola drinks as they can actually promote dehydration rather than help to prevent it. Alcoholic drinks have the same effect.
4. Check your urine to see whether your body is well hydrated – it should be pale. If your urine is dark, it contains high levels of metabolic waste

products which is a sign that you should be drinking more.

5. Don't rely on thirst as a signal for drinking. By the time you feel thirsty, your body has already accumulated high levels of sodium which is the reason you feel like a drink. As a runner your aim should be to prevent yourself from ever feeling thirsty by drinking regularly.

6. Before a race or training run you should be especially aware of how much you drink. You should drink regularly up to about 2 hours before the race starts and then take another drink about 15 minutes before the gun.

7. Once you are running, especially in hot weather, try to take in a few sips of water or sports drinks every 15 minutes or so.

8. Always try sports drinks out in training before you use them in a race. Not every drink suits every runner.

9. If you start to feel dizzy or nauseous during a race or training run, then you should stop as soon as possible. You cannot reverse the effects of dehydration and might do yourself more damage by continuing to run.

10. Make sure you are well hydrated all the time, not just when you are preparing for a race – it will give you more energy to run better times.

Are sports drinks any better than water?

Water is not only the cheapest, most readily available and most easily digested sports drink around, it is also one of the most effective. Some runners spend pounds on specialist sports drinks when they could save themselves money and time simply by turning on their kitchen tap.

Most of what you lose in sweat when you are running is fluid, and water can replace that quite adequately. Of course, sweat also contains body salts, or electrolytes, but a balanced diet after running combined with enough water will replace all of these losses.

However, in recent years, studies have shown that specialist sports drinks containing added carbohydrate can benefit some runners in some circumstances. Any endurance exercise which lasts for longer than 90 minutes, such as marathon running, can deplete an athlete's glycogen stores which, in turn, can result in the early onset of fatigue. This is when a carbohydrate sports drink taken during exercise can be useful. These drinks are formulated not only to keep you well hydrated but also to help improve your stamina.

Most of the sports drinks that you can buy contain fairly weak concentrations of carbohydrate so that it can be absorbed and used by your body as quickly as possible. Their composition means that they can be taken during exercise to provide easily absorbed carbohydrate to top up your glycogen stores and delay the onset of fatigue. In contrast, studies have shown that, for some athletes, consuming a regular high-sugar drink, such as fizzy cola or lemonade, 30–60 minutes before their race can actually hamper their running rather than help them along to faster times. Highly concentrated drinks not only take much longer to leave the stomach and reach the intestine than specialist sports drinks, but they can also contribute to hypoglycaemia, or low blood sugar levels, once you start running.

If you consume a concentrated dose of any sugary food or drink, such as a chocolate bar or orange squash, there will be a sudden increase in your blood sugar levels but, at the same time, the pancreas is triggered into releasing larger than normal doses of insulin, the hormone which controls your blood sugar by transporting it to the working muscles. Since exercise is also known to enhance this process, it is quite likely that your blood sugar will soon slump to a level much lower than it was before you took your sugar-boosting snack. Not the kind of preparation you need to run well.

It is generally agreed that some runners are more sensitive to this insulin response than others, but it is best to play safe and take a carbohydrate sports drink *during* your run or, if you must, consume your sugary snack no more than ten minutes before you start which will avoid any drop in blood sugar.

A guide to sports drinks jargon

With so many sports drinks on the market, choosing the right one can be a difficult decision to make and deciphering the jargon can be even harder. Here is a quick guide to help you choose the best drink for you:

Isotonic drinks These have approximately the same concentration as the body's own fluids which means that they are absorbed at about the same rate as water.

Hypertonic drinks These drinks are more concentrated than the body's own fluids which means that they take longer to be absorbed than water and the other sports drinks. Their main use is for extra energy throughout the day or to help replace the glycogen losses after exercise and, unlike the others, they are not designed to be taken during hard exercise.

Hypotonic drinks These drinks contain fewer dissolved particles than the body's fluids which means that they can be absorbed into the bloodstream much more quickly. It is also thought that they can increase the speed at which water is absorbed so that they help to prevent dehydration.

Energy-booster drinks Sports drinks that are marketed simply as energy drinks usually contain either glucose polymers, glucose or fructose and are formulated to replace glycogen lost through excessive exercise. These are only if you are running hard for two hours or more, but they can be useful as an energy replacer for any runner who can't face eating solids after a race.

Glucose polymers These are sometimes called maltodextrins and are short chains of glucose molecules, which means that their composition falls somewhere between that of sugar and of starch. Their biggest advantage for runners is that drinks containing glucose polymers can provide a highly concentrated form of energy as well as being easy to digest. They also taste less sweet than other drinks.

What you should eat before a race?

If there was a secret formula for the ultimate pre-race meal, most runners would pay a small fortune to find out what it was. Unfortunately there is no such recipe for success when it comes to eating to compete and every runner has different ideas about what is the perfect nutritional preparation for their big race.

The functions of a pre-race meal are to fuel your muscles with the glycogen that they need to exercise, to help prevent hypoglacaemia and to make sure that you don't start the race feeling hungry. But it should also be a psychological boost and something that you eat because you believe it works for you.

While the average runner's diet may be similar on every other day of the year, race day is different and there are no hard and fast rules about what you should eat before you start. Ask a handful of runners to describe their favourite pre-race meal and you are likely to get a different response from each of them because what they choose depends as much on the psychological benefits as anything else. In short, if you like your pre-race meal and you *think* it is giving you the edge that you need, then you are halfway there.

Of course, there are other factors determining what you eat before a race, including how far or fast you will be running and what time of day the race starts. Always have a test-run in training to make sure that you can tolerate the food you choose. Here are some guidelines to help you make sure you are ready on race day:

▶ Plan to eat your pre-race meal about 3–4 hours before you start to allow enough time for the food to digest. If you have a light meal, such as toast, it will take less time to digest and you will probably only need around two hours.

▶ A high-carbohydrate meal is the best choice – aim to include around 200–300 grams of either bread, cereal or other carbos.

▶ If you eat something less than an hour before the start it will have no effect on your glycogen stores – all it will do is stop you from feeling hungry.

▶ Avoid eating too many sugary foods which might have the effect of lowering your blood sugar levels.

▶ Avoid fatty foods which have a long transit time through the body, are difficult to digest and delay gastric emptying. That doesn't mean that you need to avoid fat altogether – some margarine on your bread, for instance, is fine.

▶ Small portions of low-fat protein, such as cottage cheese or chicken, are not too difficult to digest and can be included with your carbohydrate foods.

▶ Eat a carbohydrate-rich diet in the days leading up to the event to make sure your body is ready to race.

▶ Remember that the pre-race meal is not complete without adequate fluids.

How can you help your body to recover from exercise?

Your meal after a race or hard training session is just as important as your pre-race diet but is very often neglected by runners who simply want to relax once they have finished. There are four golden rules of successful post-exercise eating.

1. **Get plenty of rest** As strange as it seems, rest is a vital part of your nutrition programme if you have run a marathon or a very hard long-distance race! Because your glycogen stores will be depleted, your muscles will need at least two days' rest combined with a high-carbohydrate diet to recover. By doing this you'll find that your muscles won't ache or feel sore for as long as they do if you neglect your recovery programme.

2. **Replace your body salts** Because you lose electrolytes, or body salts, such as sodium and potassium, when you sweat, you will need to replace them once you have finished running. The average diet contains much more salt than we need and you should have no problem replacing sodium losses provided you eat enough food. Fruit juices, especially orange juice, are an excellent choice for replacing potassium but you might need to dilute them with water if they are too acidic for you.

3. **Replace your carbohydrates** It is especially important to eat carbohydrate-rich foods up to four hours after finishing a race or training session. As a general guideline, you will need to consume around 300kcals of carbohydrate during the two hours after you have competed and then repeat that.

4. **Keep up your fluid intake** This

should be top of your list of things to do after a race. Stick to the fluids you are used to as well as having some watery foods such as tomatoes, lettuce or other salad vegetables. Fruit juices are another good choice but avoid coffee, tea and alcohol.

Putting your nutrition plan into action

Now that you know what you are *supposed* to be eating, the next step is to make your nutrition plan work for you. This is the difficult part because it is not always easy to convert theory into practice, especially when you are leading a hectic lifestyle. Here are some solutions to the most common problems that runners face:

▶ **'I don't have time to eat breakfast'** This is no excuse for skipping the most important meal of the day. If you don't have time, make time! You can eat breakfast on the run by taking some fruit, a yoghurt or some bread with you in your bag to work. Some runners swear by dry breakfast cereal while others make themselves a sandwich the night before and eat that to start their morning. Breakfast is vital because it replenishes your glycogen stores which will be running low after not having any food since last night's meal. Don't miss it.

▶ **'I don't get home from work until 6.30p.m. and by the time I have finished my evening run it is too late to think about cooking!'** You needn't always eat a cooked meal in the evening. Why not have a high carbohydrate easy-to-prepare snack, such as beans on toast, in the evening and eat your main meal at lunchtime?

▶ **'Healthy eating is all very well if you have got the money to spend, but how can I eat healthily on a budget?'** It is a common misconception that healthy food is expensive food. In fact some of the healthiest meals you can prepare are also the cheapest. There is no better meal for a runner than a baked potato with either a tuna or cheese filling served with salad or fresh vegetables and it is also a meal to suit a tight budget. Shop around for low-fat, high-carbohydrate treats and enjoy looking for bargains!

▶ **'I don't like eating big meals and prefer to snack all day. Is that bad for me?'** No, as long as you don't snack on the wrong foods. Research shows that snacking can be better for you than three square meals a day as it provides the body with a regular supply of nutrients in easily digestible quantities. Stick to the same principles as the main nutrition plan and you will have no problems.

Women's running

At the first modern Olympic Games in 1896, there were no women competitors. In the context of the male-dominated society of the time, it was hardly surprising. What is more surprising is that it took another 88 years for the Olympic movement to allow women into the marathon. Prior to that it had been considered, with more chauvinism than hard evidence, that women were too weak and delicate to compete in distances longer than 3,000m.

Physiologically men and women are different. Men, for example, produce much higher quantities of testosterone than women. This increases the concentration of red blood cells and promotes the production of haemoglobin, the protein that carries oxygen within the cells. Men also have a VO_2max on average 10 to 12 per cent higher than women and carry much lower quantities of of body fat. These are all factors which combine to make men naturally faster than women over every distance.

But speed is not an indicator of aptitude. Women are as able to compete over long distance as any men, which has now been universally accepted, and women's distance running has finally gained the acceptance and credibility that it should always have had. While general training for any distance is more a question of ability than sex, women do have particular concerns that need to be addressed, ranging from their specialist kit to running through pregnancy.

*Running's not just good for you –
it's great for your social life.*

The female kit bag

Shoes

The question of women-only shoes is a contentious one. While most manufacturers make women's models, they tend to be cut-down versions of male designs finished in feminine colours and built on a different last, which stresses a narrower heel and midfoot. The point of dispute is whether women are biomechanically different from men. The few companies which have attempted to launch shoes designed specifically for women in the UK say they are. They contend that women's hips are wider, their legs slant towards the ground at a greater angle and their feet tend to roll inwards more. This translates into shoes which have more medial and lateral support. Unfortunately these shoes have generally performed poorly in the marketplace, providing little incentive for companies to continue developing the idea.

With one or two exceptions, you will be faced with women's models developed from their male counterparts or, if you have bigger feet, men's models only. Fit is first and foremost; if you have a narrow heel and wide forefoot look at Saucony, which makes all its shoes that way, or New Balance, which offers a variety of width fittings on most of its models. That aside follow the general shoe advice in Chapter 4.

Sports bras

Running is one of the highest impact sports on breasts. A high-quality sports specific bra is thus essential for all female runners. While that is particularly the case for large-breasted women (size C and above who need a lot of motion control), even those who feel comfortable running without a bra should avoid doing so. The breasts are supported by ligaments not muscles, which can stretch quite easily and eventually cause the breasts to irreversibly sag. That aside, a good bra will also help protect skin and draw off sweat.

There are three types of bra to consider, crop tops that compress the breasts, those that separate and a few models that do both. Crop tops are better for smaller-breasted women because of the elasticity of the materials. The weight of larger breasts will quickly break this material down and creates a rubber-band effect. Larger-breasted women often receive the best supports from bras with separate moulded cups that have minimum stretch.

You can check this by grabbing and pulling the straps and the bottom of the bra. When you try it on there should be just enough stretch to allow you to raise your arms, but that stretch should be at the back of the bra.

Even the best bras will take a beating over time so try to change them from run to run and discard them quickly if you feel they are becoming too elastic.

Finally, get the bra fitted by a specialist. According to a recent study in *Runner's World* magazine, an astonishing 70 per cent of women wear incorrectly sized and fitted bras. A specialist sports shop may be able to advise you more specifically on bras for running.

Shorts and vests

While the majority of the general clothing advice in Chapter 4 applies equally to women, there are shorts and vests on the market specifically designed for the female figure. Shorts tend to be designed with a higher waistband, a more generous cut around the hips and longer in the leg. Vests, which occasionally come with built-in sports bras, are cut higher under the arms. Finally, for those who want to use a heart-rate monitor, you can now buy a specialist sports bra with an integrated chest-band transmitter.

Period pains

As much as we try to deny it, the menstrual cycle will affect running performance. The hormonal changes within the monthly cycle not only affect mood, but can also have physical side effects such as weight gain, breast tenderness, headaches and tiredness. Most women report that the worst time to perform is just before or during their menstrual flow, a point supported by scientific research carried out in the USA. To attempt to overcome these problems follow this advice:

► Lightly stretching or exercising the abdominal area, such as sit-ups with bent knees, can help relax cramping and improve blood flow to the area.

► Drinking large amounts of water, or fruit juices which contain potassium, will help to keep bloating to a minimum. Avoid salty foods which may make you retain water.

► Eating small snacks during the day will help maintain your energy reserves. Sugary sweets, which lead to a blood sugar high followed by low, should be avoided.

► Running is a good way of balancing mood swings. So don't avoid it.

The pregnant runner

Pregnancy throws up two major questions for the committed runner – how will running affect the baby and how will pregnancy affect running performance? Certainly this is not the time to start a new training programme geared towards a major race, but you do not necessarily need to give up running altogether. Your goal should be aimed at maintaining

rather than developing fitness. You should, of course, consult your doctor if you wish to continue running.

The biggest potential danger to the foetus is through an increase in body temperature. Your core body temperature rises naturally during exercise but the process is exacerbated in the warmer spring and summer months. The main potential effect of too great an increase in the body temperature, which can easily be prevented, is damage to the foetus's central nervous system, which is especially the case during the first three months of pregnancy.

Try to limit any rise in temperature to 38.9ºC. You can do this by keeping your fluid intake high. Drink plenty of water during the day and increase it when you run. Another way of limiting potential problems is with a heart-rate monitor. Try to keep your heart rate between 140–150 bpm. Remember that one effect of endurance training is that it makes the body more capable of controlling temperature rises, so a runner who is fit before pregnancy should be in a better position than one who is not. The foetus's main energy comes from carbohydrates, so it is equally important to avoid hypoglycaemia (the lowering of blood sugar levels) during and after exercise. As you train you burn muscle and liver carbohydrate, which can be replaced by carbohydrate drinks, provided they aren't too concentrated.

Although there is very little controlled research on the effects of exercise on the foetus during pregnancy, one recent project, which followed two groups of 462 suburban women during their pregnancies, found that women who had burned more calories per week (through exercise) tended to give birth to slightly heavier babies than women who had exercised less. This implies that it is safe to exercise throughout the pregnancy and the exercise can actually be beneficial to the child's health.

The physiological stress of pregnancy may also be beneficial to the endurance runner. During the first six months, when prolonged exercise is still a relatively comfortable possibility, there are enhancements to the cardiovascular system, blood volume and haemoglobin increase and the heart pumps more blood with each beat. This significantly increases the overall supply to the tissues, thus giving a greater supply of oxygen, which leads to enhanced endurance performance.

These effects are caused by hormonal changes during pregnancy and will continue until 20–24 weeks after gestation. The anabolic effects that take place after pregnancy can lead to increases in both strength and endurance.

Women's nutrition

The optimum diet for female runners is rooted in good well-balanced basics centred on carbohydrates, proteins and fats. But women generally need more calcium, iron and folic acid than men.

Calcium builds strong bones and when calcium intake is low, bones grow thin because of reduced calcium deposits (osteoporosis). When oestrogen levels rise, because of intense training, the menopause or amenorrhea, the risk of osteoporosis rises. To combat osteoporosis women between 25–50 should try to take in 800 milligrams of calcium a day, which is three to four servings of calcium-rich foods like milk, yoghurt, cheese, tofu, sardines, salmon, spinach or broccoli.

Iron is important in red blood cells and helps to deliver oxygen to all cells of the body. Menstruating women need greater supplies of iron than men. You can increase iron intake by eating lean

Five good reasons for women to run

1. Running helps to produce healthy skin. According to dermatologists, running stimulates circulation, transports nutrients and flushes out waste products. All of this leads to a reduction in subcutaneous fat, making the skin clearer.

2. Running women produce a far less potent form of oestrogen than their sedentary counterparts. As a result, female runners cut by half their risks of developing breast and uterine cancer and by two-thirds their risk of contracting the form of diabetes that most commonly plagues women.

3. Heart disease kills three times as many women each year as breast cancer. One of the best ways of fighting that disease is with exercise; it lowers your blood pressure and resting heart rate, raises your levels of good HDL cholesterol and helps you to maintain a healthy weight.

4. Fast running burns more calories than slow running but slow running burns more calories than just about any other activity. Nothing will help you to lose weight and keep it off the way running does.

5. Exploring your competitive side can offer benefits beyond running. Racing can help you to tap into a goal-setting, assertive and self-disciplined side of your personality. These attributes can boost your potential for success in other parts of your life, such as your career.

cuts of red meat, bread and cereals that are iron-fortified or taking a multi-vitamin supplement that includes iron. Also avoid drinking too much coffee or tea and eat tomatoes or orange juice with iron-rich foods. Acidic solutions aid iron absorption.

Women who are contemplating pregnancy need folic acid, which can be found in oranges, spinach and green vegetables.

Weight loss

Many women first start running to keep their weight under control. While a combination of sensible eating and running is the best way to lose weight, you will lose weight quicker by increasing the amount of exercise you do rather than restricting the amount of food you take in. The less you eat the more your

Running is the simplest way to get fit and lose weight.

body adapts to eating less, but when you maintain your food intake and increase the exercise your body will increasingly turn on its fat reserves to fuel that exercise. Here are a few basic but often forgotten points to remember when trying to lose weight.

▶ The basic principle of weight loss is that you have to take in less calories than your body uses in energy. It will then turn to the energy reserves, stored as fat, to fuel those demands.

▶ Exercise may make you lose your appetite, but only temporarily. This is usually linked to a rise in body temperature, and is less likely to happen when running in colder conditions when any temperature drop may actually make you hungrier.

▶ Eat early rather than late. Late-night bingeing, common among crash diets, gives your body little time to work off the calories you are taking in.

▶ Snacking is not wrong. Snacking on the wrong foods – crisps, biscuits and sweets high in sugars and fat – is. Hunger is natural – respond to it by putting high-quality food into your body.

▶ While controlling your intake of fat is important, it is overall calories that count. Excess carbohydrate or protein in diet will also be converted to fat.

The last word on safety

It is a sad reality of modern life that lone females are more likely to be attacked while out running than men. While such an eventuality is statistically very remote, women should be aware of the dangers and avoid doing stupid things which make them more vulnerable. Running as part of a group; avoiding unfamiliar or enclosed areas, particularly after dark; being aware of people around you; not wearing a personal stereo and varying your routes regularly should all be a common-sense part of your running routine. Carrying an attack alarm, a small battery-operated box, which emits a loud ear-piercing shrill, may make you feel more confident.

If you think you are being followed head towards light, people or crowds. If you are going to be attacked it won't be in front of other people. In the unlikely event that you are approached while out running, avoid confronting your attacker. While you may feel confident of landing a well-aimed foot to the groin, if you miss you could be in trouble. Your best defence is your speed so use that adrenaline to run away.

Five things for female runners to remember

1. Women sweat less than men, but they dissipate heat just as well. That's because women are smaller and have a higher body-surface-to-volume ratio, which means that, although their evaporative cooling is less efficient, they need less of it to achieve the same result.

2. Morning is the best time for women to run. Statistically it's the safest time: women are more likely to be attacked later in the day. Studies have also shown that morning exercisers are more likely to stick with it,

plus it gives you a feeling of accomplishment, which is a great way to start the day!

3. Trying to lose weight by eating less and running more doesn't work. The more you exercise and the less you eat the more likely your body is to 'hibernate'. That means you'll conserve calories and thwart your efforts to lose fat. The better bet is to exercise reasonably and increase your food intake early in the day to fuel your training.

4. Babies dislike the taste of

post-exercise milk which is high in lactic acid and imparts a sour flavour. If you are breast feeding, either collect milk for later feeding or breast feed before running.

5. Running outdoors with headphones is a serious safety hazard. You won't be able to hear cars, cyclists or someone approaching who intends to do you harm. Attackers will always pick a victim who looks vulnerable, which is exactly how someone with headphones looks.

Club athletics

Running is a great sport if you're looking to get fit – it's cheap and you don't necessarily need other people – but you may find that, in order to progress as you'd like, and to add a social dimension to your training, joining a running club is your next step.

Britain has the most envied athletics club system in the world. Almost every town in Britain has an athletics club and the larger cities a wide variety – in London, close to fifty!

Cost varies greatly, but joining an athletics or running club is usually a lot cheaper than an average tennis or squash club. Subscriptions tend to vary from £10 to £40 per annum, with sometimes an extra £1 or so for using the facilities.

Most clubs have coaches or access to coaching facilities. This is particularly vital for anyone wishing to try any technical events such as sprinting but even distance runners can benefit from coaching advice and technique work. Larger clubs should have a number of coaches, and may have specialist areas, say for sprints, middle-distance, long-distance and young athletes.

Additionally, many athletics clubs have

Join a club and you need never run alone.

training groups at the local track. Quite often they are split as per ability and some make special efforts to cater for beginners. Beware, though, some clubs just may not be suitable if you are a 10-minute miler.

Most running clubs also have club training nights when large groups of runners go for a social run together – at least, that's how the run starts out!

Most athletic clubs are based at a local track, or have an arrangement with a local authority for use of changing rooms and a club house. The newer breed of running club tends to meet in a park or local sports club or even a pub or member's house. Even if you can't find a suitable group to run with, it should be possible to find individual training partners or club members who live in your locality or neighbourhood.

Some runners join a club for the social scene as much as the training. Clubs often put on a variety of social events and, with such a common bond, club runners tend to get on well amongst themselves, even if it does sometimes end up with discussions of the next race.

A real benefit of joining a club is the competition. Most running clubs are affiliated to various cross-country leagues or associations and provide the budding cross-country runner with numerous competitions. From October through to March, whatever your age or sex, the club runner will probably get the choice of taking part in four area leagues, a county, area and national championship, together with four or five other regionalised races and a few relays, and it might not cost you a penny, bar the travel costs. Most clubs pay a simple fee to be affiliated to the league or association and, as you are representing your club, do not pass the cost on to the runner.

Organized competition is where clubs excel.

If you want to join a club, what can you do?

The best way of finding a suitable club is to ring the area association (see useful numbers list). The various areas (South, North, Midlands, Wales, N. Ireland & Scotland) hold details of all registered clubs within the area and can give you information on the nearest and most suitable club within your county or locality.

They should supply you with a telephone number or address of the club's membership secretary, who will then probably send you a membership form and details of the club. It's probably worth turning up at a club night before you join, just to see if it really is suitable for you.

Before you arrive for your first visit, think of all the questions you need to ask (e.g. how much does it cost per session, or does it cater for slower runners?) and make sure a club official answers them to your satisfaction before you pay your initial subscription.

If you like what you see and hear, enquire about club vests. If you take part in any club competition, you could end up getting your team disqualified if you don't wear the officially registered club colours and it's probably worth ordering a vest when you join, rather than trying to get hold of one the day before you make your club debut.

Warning: if you do make an unwise choice of what club you join and then find a more suitable one, it isn't just a case of changing your membership and club vest. In fact, it can be a more laborious task to

leave a club than it is to join one!

The sport operates a policy that many regard as somewhat archaic and inflexible, and changing clubs with effect for competition can take up to nine months. This is primarily to stop athletes from smaller clubs being poached by larger, more successful clubs or runners changing clubs every week.

For athletes moving into a new area or runners who have extremely good reasons for leaving, each area association has a hardship committee to discuss each case. Note this also applies if you join a second club and then decide you would prefer to run for the newer one instead.

One of the most enjoyable aspects of competition within a club is the road and cross-country relay. They are an excellent way of fostering club spirit and, for once, you won't be competing against your clubmates but with them. One advantage over normal races is that they provide a variety of races and you can be passing or being overtaken by runners you wouldn't normally be up against in your particular field. Apart from some long-distance events, most relays are run over short distances and suit newcomers. Many clubs enter a number of teams and these are selected by ability: you may end up in the G or H team on your relay debut.

In most clubs, the out-and-out club road runner doesn't tend to get quite as much benefit as the cross-country or relay runner and in most cases will have to enter races separately and pay whatever the entry fee is themselves. On the plus side, though, all unaffiliated or unattached runners have to pay an extra £1, which is collected by each race organiser and is then paid to the association to which the race is affiliated. This means club runners receive a £1 race reduction in their entry fees and a frequent race competitor will soon cancel out most of his subscription fee.

It's not just financially that a club runner gains. A runner who may not be of a sufficiently high standard to

What should you get from your club?

After applying for membership, most clubs hold election meetings (in most cases just a formality, running clubs are certainly less restrictive than golf clubs).

Once the committee have confirmed your membership, you should receive a letter from the membership secretary, together with a list of club rules and a current fixture list. You should also receive a list of club officers and where you can get a stock of club kit from. Most clubs have secretaries for both road, track and cross-country, a social secretary, and a men's and women's captain. If you have a particular interest, you should contact the relevant parties. In theory, some club officers may contact you but as most club committee members or officers probably have full-time jobs and are active athletes themselves, they might take a while to get in touch.

Larger clubs will probably have some form of magazine or newsletter, detailing results and news and upcoming events. When it comes to leagues and events such as championships, in some cases the club will ask you to compete, but, again, some clubs rely on the individual to offer their services first.

---

challenge for individual awards, may have the opportunity of team prizes or medals. Most road races award prizes or trophies for up to the first three teams in a category decided by totals of scoring runners (smallest total winning) and in the majority of races go to runners who finish well behind the individual award winners. Apart from geographically based clubs, there are specialist clubs such as the Road Runners Club (RRC) and the 100K Association for ultra runners.

The RRC has thousands of members and is an ideal organisation for the newcomer to road running to join for a modest annual subscription. Apart from extensive fixture lists, they publish seasonal newsletters and have a standards scheme, which can act as a good incentive to improve.

Another organisation that is worth considering if you have a particular interest in longer races is the Fell Racing Association (FRA). This form of competition (known as hill running in Scotland) is very popular in the North and Scotland, Wales and Northern Ireland. If you want to take part in fell racing in England and Wales, you must join the FRA. For a fairly modest fee, you will receive a very detailed fixture list and an extensive magazine covering the sport. Note, though, this is not a sport for an inexperienced runner or someone with no experience of being on a mountain.

While most clubs do make a special effort to recruit women, and indeed there are some all-women clubs, women should also think of joining the *Runner's World*/Reebok Sisters Network. For just a £5 fee, members receive a T-shirt, newsletter and information on their nearest women's running group.

Track running

It is even more important to join a club if you are concentrating on shorter track events. Almost every club that actively pursues a track and field programme belongs to an area league. It should be noted a number of road running clubs don't cater for track running and runners will need to join another club second claim (first claim on the track).

While there are high-quality National Leagues, which over the years have included competitors such as Daley Thompson, Linford Christie, Seb Coe and Steve Ovett, it is in the area leagues that most club athletes will get to compete. The Midlands, Northern and Southern areas plus Wales, Scotland and Northern Ireland have their own leagues, both men's and women's.

The biggest is the Southern League, which has twenty-five teams in eight divisions. There are six rounds of fixtures per year, with each division having five matches, with five teams per match. This means every team gets to face their rivals in the league in one match per year.

Each fixture has around twenty events, with each club providing two per event (four in the two relays) with nominated A and B strings. The standard varies greatly from Division 1 to Division 8. On the whole, the lower the division, the lower the standard, and most clubs in the lower divisions only manage to cover all the events with their athletes taking part in a number of disciplines. So you may want to run the 100m or 5,000m but don't be surprised if you get asked to fill in with a steeplechase or triple jump! Standards in the lower divisions of all areas are not particularly high and a newcomer shouldn't feel too out of his depth, and just by finishing you will be scoring points for your club.

While the leagues are regionalised, it can in rare instances involve a team from Suffolk travelling to Cornwall for a match, but that just adds to the sense of adventure and *esprit de corps*.

Some counties have their own leagues and there are also some very popular young athletes' leagues.

Most clubs provide extra competition in the form of their own club championships. One form of competition that is open to all runners, whether they

Ten good reasons to join a club

1. Coaching.
2. Competition.
3. Social functions.
4. Training partners.
5. Reduced race fees.
6. Information.
7. Additional places in the London Marathon.
8. You are ineligible to compete in cross-country or track races after a year of being 'unattached'.
9. Training facilities.
10. Camaraderie at races and increased prize-winning opportunities.

are a member of a club or not, is the open graded meeting, which is advertised at the local track or in the local press. These events are usually graded on past performances, with the fastest runners at any discipline all competing in one race, and the slowest in another, and most meetings will have at least one sprint and one middle-distance distance.

Note, though, that officially unattached runners can only compete in track (and cross-country) events for one year before they must join a club.

Useful telephone numbers

AA of Wales Office
(01792 456237)

British Athletic Federation
(0121 440 5000)

British Triathlon Association
(01530 414234)

British Veterans Athletic Federation
(0181 683 2602)

Fell Running Association
(01539 731012)

Midland Counties AA
(0121 452 1500)

Northern Ireland AA Office
(01232 381222)

North of England AA Office
(01132 461835)

Road Runner's Club
(01438 716508)

Runner's World magazine
(0171 291 6000)

Runner's World/Reebok Sisters Network
(write to PO Box 76, Warrington,
Cheshire WA4 2FB)

Scottish Athletic Federation
(0131 317 7320)

South of England AA Office
(0171 247 2963)

Trail Running Association
(01488 648671)

The triathlon

The evolutionary process that turns a runner into a triathlete or duathlete is usually sparked by one of two phenomena: the first is a feeling of having been there and done that in running terms and wanting to try something different. The second is injury, which might force a runner into using the non-weight-bearing sports of cycling or swimming to maintain fitness, and deciding to continue to include those other sports in their training programme once the injury has healed.

For whatever reasons a runner might get into triathlon, he or she will be faced with a new set of training factors and principles. The first and most obvious change is the inclusion of two other sports (swimming and cycling) in the case of triathlon and one additional sport (cycling) for duathletes in one's sporting life. New hardware has to be bought and training has to be modified to accommodate the extra workload.

An ordinary racing bike can work for novice triathletes.

The hardware

A so-called triathlon bike isn't an absolute necessity for someone who has decided to try triathlon, but looked at from a runner's point of view it is a wise investment. Triathlon bikes have steeper angles than conventional road-racing bikes. These geometric changes shift the triathlete's position slightly forward, thus opening the angle between the torso and the thigh and, all else being well, achieving an optimally efficient riding position.

Runners who are new to cycling can usually achieve a near-optimal flat-back, aerodynamic position on the bike by adopting one of the forward positions that triathlon bikes impose. You can often achieve the same effect by playing with the saddle position, height and handlebar stem on a conventional bike. A forward cycling position will help to rotate the pelvis forward and down, which will give you better leg extension and smoother pedalling. It will also allow you to ride with a higher saddle position than conventional road-racing cyclists, a factor thought to facilitate the bike-to-run transition. Finally, it is a quicker and easier way of training your body to adopt the optimal riding position, something many runners have a problem with. The alternative is years of cycle training, and that's not an acceptable option for the impatient or part-time budding triathlete.

Once you become more experienced as a triathlete, you might find that you can comfortably maintain your aerodynamic position on a classically angled bike without discomfort. Cycling purists say that classic is preferable, if your riding position is better, as it affords a greater power output.

The other characteristic of triathlon bikes that sets them apart from traditional road bikes is aero handlebars.

These were originally developed in the quest for ever-improved aerodynamics, and their principles are borrowed from the downhill skier's tuck position. Set up and used correctly, aerobars should result in the ever-desirable flat back and a narrower frontal area on the rider, without forfeiting control. By lowering or lengthening your stem, you can flatten your back and enhance your aerodynamics, too.

If you want to try triathlon but don't want to fork out more than you paid for your car for a bike, go for a lightweight conventional road-race frame or one of the mid-range triathlon bikes that are on today's market. Play with saddle position and stem length until you feel comfortable in as aerodynamic a position as you can muster, and work at improving on it with time. Remember that with every movement of your upper body, you create turbulence when you ride, and that slows you down, so you want to find a position that you can hold for long periods.

If you choose to go for a conventional bike, upgrade it progressively by investing in tri-spoke wheels (more aerodynamic than conventional spoked wheels) and by adding aerobars. One final note that might affect the type of bike you choose is that if you don't naturally adopt the optimal, flat-back position on a bike, you could well be slower when riding on aerobars than you would be on ordinary drop handlebars.

Swimming requires a less significant investment in hardware than cycling, but you'll still need to buy yourself some equipment. The minima are non-glare, anti-mist goggles; a racing swimsuit (Bermuda shorts or bikinis produce too much drag in the water); and, if you plan to race in northern Europe, a wetsuit, which should be cut specially for swimming and should be no more than

5mm thick. Training accessories that runners who take up swimming often find useful are pullbuoys (small floats that you hold between your legs, permitting you to propel yourself forward through the water using arms only); hand-paddles to strengthen the upper body; and kickboards.

The training

All of triathlon's component sports will train your cardiovascular system, so even if you cut back on your running mileage to add swimming and cycling sessions to your weekly programme, you shouldn't lose aerobic fitness. Swimming is the least demanding of triathlon's disciplines in physiological terms, but the most demanding technically. Running is at the opposite end of the scale: the level of skill isn't too elevated; the injury and fatigue risk is.

When you are devising your triathlon

Swimming is the most technically demanding aspect of triathlon.

training schedule allow more recovery time for running sessions than swimming or cycling sessions. Sensibly managed, triathlon will allow you to carry a much greater training load without running a concurrently higher risk of injury.

Most of the time you spend in triathlon training will probably be devoted to cycling, with running in second place and swimming in third. The training effect of a 45-minute running session is greater than equal time in the pool or on the bike. Former Olympic Marathon champion Frank Shorter, who became a world class duathlete when injury tried to curtail his running career, reckons that he had to cycle for 45 minutes to an hour with his pulse-rate maintained at a steady 140 beats per minute to get the same training effect as he would derive from a six- to seven-mile run. If you establish your own training equivalents for each of triathlon's sports you'll be able to substitute an equivalent swim session for a run on days when running proves impossible. Don't entirely replace one sport with another, though: to become a good cyclist, you need to cycle to accustom your muscles to the way they're expected to function on a bike. To become a good triathlete, you need to swim, cycle and run.

Base your training for all three sports on the type of triathlon you plan to do and its timing in the season calendar. If you're hoping to get a place in the top ten in an international Olympic distance triathlon (1,500m swim/40-kilometre bike/10-kilometre run) you should plan a training schedule that includes more threshold and speedwork and less distance work than someone who is training to finish an Ironman distance race (2.4-mile swim/112-mile bike/26.2-mile run). Having chosen your event, follow the same training principles as outlined in other sections of this book, striking a good balance between sprint, VO$_2$max, AT and aerobic work.

Finding enough time to train for three sports, while continuing to live a normal life, is tricky. Some triathletes train three times a day: a bike ride in the morning, run at lunchtime and swim in the afternoon. But you don't have to train at every discipline, every day. Focus on your weakest of the three sports, which as a runner is likely to be either swimming or cycling. Most of a new triathlete's swimming time should be spent perfecting technique, while new cyclists should concentrate on getting used to the bike and building an endurance base. Once you are reasonably competent at the two new sports, concoct a mixed training programme, similar to your running one, i.e. with fartlek, hill sessions on the bike and sprints in the pool.

Many triathletes tend to run four to five times a week, cycle five times, and swim three to four times weekly. It might sound a lot, but that sort of workload is accessible to most without abandoning all notions of a social and family life, and without incurring too high an injury risk. Just how you lay out your training schedule will depend largely on pool

	Swim	Bike	Run
Monday	Club a.m.	Rest	Lunchtime: 10–15K with fartlek or hills
Tuesday	Rest	Morning ride: 40K with hills	Rest
Weds	Club a.m.	Evening: turbo/gym	Evening: cross-train with bike training. Back-to-back session
Thursday	Club p.m. or rest	Ride to work and back – steady a.m., fartlek p.m.	Lunchtime: track
Friday	Club a.m. or rest	Rest or easy commute	Rest
Saturday	Rest	Long ride	Rest
Sunday	Rest	Med-distance ride followed by …	LSD run

times and opportunities for cycling in your area.

There is a fourth event in triathlons that you should also train for: the transition. Back-to-back training, or moving from one sport directly into another, will go some way to helping you to accustom your body to transitions and minimise the time you spend in the transition area. The most useful back-to-back session for a triathlete consists of going directly from a bike ride into a running session. This is the most difficult transition in triathlon, and by practising it in training, you will get used to the sensations associated with it and learn to cope better with them. Before you embark on back-to-back training, though, build a good base by following a swim, bike and run training programme for at least six weeks. Then, do just one back-to-back session a week. You probably won't want to subject yourself to the unpleasantness of getting off the bike and going straight into a run any more than that, anyway.

The transition area itself might seem like a great place to have a little rest, but the goal of the competitive triathlete should be to get in and out of there as quickly as possible. To facilitate that, try:

► Laying out your kit in the order that you'll be putting it on, with any food and drink you'll be using on the bike and run sections already in place either on the bike or in your jersey or bumbag pockets

► Memorising the transition area by walking from the swim exit to your bike rack; from the bike entry to the bike rack, etc.

► Adding visual aids to your bike-rack space, to help you find your steed more quickly. Use large, immobile landmarks (not the dirigible that's filming the race) to get a bearing on your transition-area space.

► Leaving your bike shoes clipped into your pedals and slipping your feet into them on the bike course. This takes a bit of practice …

► Using lace-locks on your running shoes.

Swimming

The stroke favoured by triathletes is front crawl, as it derives 90 per cent of its forward propulsion from the arms, thus sparing the legs for the demands of cycling and running. Being a good swimmer depends largely on technique, and the best way to learn good swimming technique is to join a triathlon club's swim sessions. There, you should learn the following:

► The hand's entry into the water should be clean: slice your hand diagonally into the water as if you are inserting a knife into jelly. Then, extend the arm forward.

► Grab the water and visualise pulling yourself over it. Your hand should trace a gentle S underwater and your elbow should always be bent (with the exception of when you extend your arm forward, above), even when you carry the arm out of the water for the recovery phase.

► During the recovery phase, maintain a high elbow. Visualise that you are a marionette, with a string attached to your elbow, and that the puppeteer is carrying your arm forward using an arc motion.

► Your head should break the water roughly at your hairline. If your head position is correct, you'll be able to breathe in the bow wave that you create when you swim, and you will have a streamlined position in the water, too. If your head is too high, your legs will compensate by being too low in the water, creating drag.

► The front-crawl kick acts as a rudder, contributing little to forward propulsion. Save your legs for the next two events.

- Breathing should come naturally during swimming – just as it does in running. Exhale gently when your face is first underwater, punctuating the exhalation with a little more force just before you turn your head to one side to breath. Your face should be out of the water, allowing you to breathe, when your arm is in the recovery phase.
- During races, you may compete in an open-water swim. For this, it's useful to be able to breathe bilaterally, e.g. on both sides. Practise this skill in the pool.
- You'll need to get your bearings from time to time in an open-water swim – there are no black lines along the bottom of the sea! Every fifth stroke or so, deepen your stroke a bit and raise your head forwards, water-polo style, to check that you're still on the right course. You should have visually noted some landmarks, both on shore and in the water, before the race. Don't rely on following the swimmer in front of you: they might be lost, too!

Cycling

Although less technical than swimming, there are some aspects of cycling that require practice, and the perfection of which will make you a better triathlete.

- Think 'round' not 'up-and-down' when you pedal. A good visual aid to achieve round pedalling is to imagine that you are scraping bubble gum off the bottom of your shoe: the action of the foot and ankle isn't too far removed from the action that you'd

make with your wrist and hand if you were stroking a cat. Your ankles should flex and extend throughout the pedal stroke.

- Every time you move your upper body on the bike, you are creating turbulence which will slow you down. So you should aim to find a position on the bike which will allow you to have as flat a back as possible, with as small a frontal area exposition as possible (the optimum is to have your forearms touching along their entire length, but that sacrifices too much control). Find what's most comfortable for you and grow into the ultimate triathlete's position. Remember: you have to run after your ride.
- Always wear a helmet. Not only are they required by the rules, but they could also save your noggin in a serious accident. The right helmet can make you more aerodynamic, too.
- Cycling gloves are more than just a sponsor's way of getting their branding onto another part of your body: they'll protect your hands if you happen to come off.
- Clipless pedals are virtually standard these days, and they help you to pedal more efficiently. Some clipless pedal systems allow for lateral movement; others are immobile. If you have knee problems, seek advice on which pedal system is best for you, trying a few, if at all possible. It's not necessarily going to be the moveable pedals that suit your knees best. Ask an expert for help when setting up your cleat position on the shoe, and when you first ride with clipless pedals, adjust them so that you can release your feet easily.

Index